A KINGSTON LACY CHILDHOOD

Reminiscences of
VIOLA BANKES

Collected by Pamela Watkin

THE DOVECOTE PRESS

First published in 1986 by The Dovecote Press Ltd
Stanbridge, Wimborne, Dorset BH21 4JD

ISBN 0 946159 33 5

© Pamela Watkin 1986

Printed and bound in Great Britain by
Biddles Ltd, Guildford and King's Lynn

7   9   8

For Tim, Toby and the two Lalages

Contents

Foreword

'Why did you write the book in the first person?' you may ask, 'The story is not your story; the style too full of modernisms to be that of Viola Bankes.' Yet right from the start the use of the first person seemed the only way to turn the many hours of conversation with Viola Bankes into a story that would catch the spontaneity of her memories, and evoke the spirit of the Kingston Lacy she had known as a child. But this is not an autobiography, and I must make that clear.

I should like to thank Viola Bankes for having generously allowed me to question and cross-question her and for her forbearance in tolerating distortions which must inevitably have crept into this account, at second-hand, of her childhood over half a century ago.

I am grateful for help from the National Trust, Edward Dukes, formerly Head Gardener at Kingston Lacy, Dr Cynthia Gabriel, Kenneth Curtis, The Wills Library, Guy's Hospital, the British Museum and Eric J. Freeman, Librarian of The Wellcome Institute for the History of Medicine. I also remember with gratitude my mother, my friendly critic at every stage, who has not lived to see the published volume.

PAMELA WATKIN

1
Antecedents

As the car drew up at my old home, Kingston Lacy, nothing seemed to have changed except me. My family, the Bankes of Kingston Lacy and Corfe Castle, had continued to live there comfortably, as they had done for three centuries, until my brother's recent death. Stocky, mahogany-coloured Red Devon cattle still munched away on the hummocky grass under the platformed branches of the ancient cedars, and the stately, grey-green mansion kept watch over its smooth lawns. Now, in old age, I remembered the day, over fifty years before, when I had renounced it all for ever.

My mother had been confident that our superior background and education, particularly after all the balls she had laboriously given for us year after year, would equip my sister, Daphne, and me to carry off in triumph, not only the Duke of Hamilton but even the Prince of Wales himself. In fact, Daphne never married, all her engagements having been broken off by my mother who subjected her daughter's unfortunate fiancés to severe scrutiny and eventually pronounced every one to be unsuitable.

Now, to make matters worse, on this spring morning in 1927, I myself was engaged not to a Knight of the Realm, a Prince of the Blood Royal nor to a Duke, but to a highly qualified, charming and cultured doctor. Unless a doctor had already risen so high in his profession as to be knighted he would be considered a very unimportant person at Kingston Lacy, no account being taken of his learning and dedication or of how we would all hang on his every word in a crisis. What seemed even worse, in those outrageously prejudiced days, was that the doctor I had chosen to marry was Australian. The rift which my other provoking friendships had opened between my mother and me widened irrevocably. The doors of her London house were already closed to me. Now, unless I had a change of heart, I was also to be banned from her country home.

I had spent the previous day angrily tossing all the possessions I could really call my own into trunks: clothes, shoes, books, jewellery. They clattered off to Wimborne Station in the wagonette and it only remained to say goodbye. Tense with irritation and distress, smiling brightly at the servants, I clicked briskly down the white Carrara marble stairs, carrying what would turn out to be the last present my mother would ever give me, my favourite blue leather case, which was lined with green silk and has my initials, V.F.B., on it in gold.

I faced her in the lofty entrance hall, blatantly à la mode in my cloche hat, fox fur, and slim-fitting heavy silk coat, fastened with one big button at the waist. I tried to feel some sympathy for her, so unbending and unloving in her inevitable black, ruffled taffeta blouse with its diamond clasp, tiny half inch white collar and cuffs and black serge skirt. The fine oval bone structure of her face, which had made her seem so beautiful when she used to lean over my bed in the nursery, had now disappeared.

If she had held out her hand to me, or shown the slightest weakness, I might, at the very last moment, have hesitated, but her large, prominent hazel eyes stared ruthlessly at me from her stern, white face, with icy disapproval. We said a stiff goodbye, then I shook hands with the old butler, Mr. Cooper. With my mother watching, I could not throw my arms round his neck as I longed to do. I marched determinedly through the wide stone porch and down the steps to the drive where the chauffeur held open the door of the dark blue Wolseley car. Then we drove away.

At the Wimborne Lodge, Mr Shears, the wife of the woodcutter, a bearded man with a perpetual drip on his nose, pulled open the heavy wrought iron gate between the two grey pillars my mother had had erected, her lips moving in her usual envious greeting:

'Nice to be you!' she called, as the car turned into the lane. She could not know that this would be the last time she would ever greet me or even consider me to be particularly lucky.

Outside, in the everyday world, life went on just as usual. A tall, good-looking lad, one of the many children of my mother's farming tenant, Fred Richards, looked up from scything the long grass to wave to me. Two school boys in knee-length shorts played 'last across the lane' just before the car reached them. A carter, trundling towards Kingston Lacy with a load of fish (the only food the estate itself could not supply), touched his hat as if this was just an ordinary day.

Now, in 1981, continuing the feud begun so long ago, my brother, Ralph, had made a bequest of the sixteen thousand acre estates of Corfe Castle, the Isle of Purbeck and Kingston Lacy, together with the Bankes collection of pictures, to the National Trust. He had left nothing at all to me. How would I react to seeing the lawns where we had chased each other, or strolled with friends, or climbed the chestnut trees?

It was, after all, a whole lifetime away.

2
Nursery Days

To begin at the beginning: I had never had any grand-parents as far as I remember, but, like Topsy, 'just growed'. I never met or was told anything about my father's parents, Edmund Bankes and his wife, and my mother was just as reticent about her own parents as she was about everything else in her unaccountably secret past.

I would have loved to experience the warm affection of a grandmother or grandfather, especially since my father died when I was four and my mother's love towards me was frequently difficult to discern behind her severe exterior. All I ever found out was that William Thomson Fraser, my mother's Scottish father, was Consul in Java. His wife, my grandmother, was Dutch, a member of a Van Onnen family.

Henrietta Jenny Fraser, my mother, was, before she married, a well-known international beauty. She had perfectly white, straight teeth and big hazel eyes which, despite her later severity towards my sister and me, in those days shone with a goodness and charm which, people said, sometimes deepened into a seraphic radiance. Hers was not a greyhound figure. She was always very full in the bosom, which was much admired in Victorian and Edwardian days. In fashionable Ostende and in Homburg, the Spa which gave its name to the soft felt hat sported there by King Edward VII, people stood on their chairs to watch "la belle Anglaise" go by.

It was not surprising that my father, Walter Ralph Bankes,

though hotly pursued by all the aristocratic mothers of England for his riches, breeding and good looks, when seeking a suitable mistress of Kingston Lacy, should select her for his bride. On her part, the fact that he was an Englishman, in addition to all his other charms, physical and financial, was enticing: she had previously nearly caused an international incident by refusing to marry a mediatised German Prince.

Walter Ralph Bankes, Squire of Kingston Lacy, hereditary Lord High Admiral of Purbeck, Mayor of Corfe Castle by Royal Charter, Lay Bishop of Wimborne and Justice of the Peace, was also intriguing because he had travelled widely. His broad-shouldered figure and aquiline features were as well known in the opera houses of Italy and the ballrooms of Paris as in the fields and woods of Dorset. Experience had matured him and his brooding eyes suggested a dangerous sophistication, which contrasted irresistibly with the open smiles of younger men. My mother was so taken with him when she met him, in a country house in England, that, as she went up the wide oak staircase to the room, she confided to her lady's maid, 'That is the man I shall marry.'

The wedding took place in 1895, at fashionable St George's Church, Hanover Square. Even before the couple left London, the excited tenants of the estate were already lining the route from Wimborne Station to Kingston Lacy, awaiting their arrival. The Victoria, a low, light, four-wheeled carriage with a folding hood, stood waiting with the coachman. The horses were decorated with flowers and the carriage sparkled with paint and polish. All was ready for the new master and mistress of Kingston Lacy to alight from the ponderous steam train. The church in London had been elegantly dazzling, men wearing glittering uniforms, the ladies in gorgeous gowns. Here, in the twisting, leafy lanes of Dorset, gathered chattering young tenants' wives in their best hats and cotton frocks, rosy little girls in starched white dresses and frilly bonnets and boys from the estate villages, some wearing neat sailor suits and looking unnaturally clean; others more relaxed and dusty in cut down, clumsy tweeds. Old women in hand-knitted shawls and serviceable long serge skirts stood reminiscing about the days when the young squire was a child:

'No more than six or seven and still had a kind word for everyone.' The head gardener, usually sternly occupied in the serious business of growing plants and fruit, was smiling with satisfaction as he thought that soon the Squire's lady would be enjoying the fresh sweet fragrance of flowers that filled every room in the big house.

As the carriage appeared, a cheer went up, reaching its climax at the entrance to the park. The waiting crowd surged forward, so that my alarmed parents wondered if the tenants would all be mown down or if they would overturn the Victoria and spill out their popular employers into the mud. However, two grooms unhitched the alarmed carriage horses; 'Truth' (badly named, for she had a tendency to prance round in circles ever since she had had sun-stroke) and 'Topsy', usually very well-mannered but rolling her eyes nervously at the unaccustomed fuss. Stable boys, stalwart farmers and muscular ploughmen took a grip on the shafts and enthusiastically pulled the carriage themselves. Wives and children tagged on behind the whole cheering procession as it flowed up the winding drive between the trees to the steps before the main entrance.

There was only scarcely less exuberance than when my father had driven his fascinatingly notorious friend, Lily Langtry, along the road to Wimborne, while curious crowds pressed round. But, at any rate, here was a beautiful lady who surely would provide them with an heir. The tenants often worried that my father, who was already forty-four and very loath to settle down, would die before he could father a son and so let the property pass to a distant cousin who would not have the same warmly paternal interest in them.

It was not too long before babies began to appear. We were all born in London as my mother would not trust country doctors for such important events. First, in 1898, came my fair, fat little sister, Daphne. We were proudly told that the great dramatic actress, Sarah Bernhardt (in plumed hat and scarlet riding habit, riding a beautiful white horse, I always liked to imagine) spotting her being pushed in her pram in Hyde Park by her nursery maid and nurse, remarked, with histrionic admiration, 'Ah! Quel amour de petit bébé!'

Adorable or not, Daphne, was, nevertheless, not a boy. Nor, equally inconveniently, was I.

A premature, dark-complexioned baby, I had no one to love me but Jo-Jo, a sweet-natured, German girl, my mother's companion. In her soft but guttural voice, she coaxed my sorrowing, humiliated mother and my angry father into at least acknowledging my existence while they awaited the baby boy who would prove that their union had not been in vain.

I had been born on February 11th, 1900, but nine months slipped by before, on November 29th, my father, W. R. Bankes, J. P. for Dorsetshire (as entered on the certificate) bothered to register my birth in the St George sub-district of Belgrave in the County of London. He had wanted to call me Pansy, perhaps after one of his lady friends, for there were scores of photographs of pretty women with masses of piled up hair, tiny waists, rounded bosoms and bulging bustles, in his heavy, red leather, gold-tooled, brass-clasped album.

'Could this be Pansy?' I wondered later, peering in its pages at a coyly pretty lady in a straw hat with lace gown, parasol and silk flowers. Or was it this lady, all Boa, organdie and feathers? I did not think any of them attractive enough to rival my beautiful mother.

My mother countered his suggestion with one of her own, Violet, and they compromised with Viola Florence. Had they read *Twelfth Night*? A third name, Agnes, mysteriously crept onto the birth certificate too. Was she also a dying or dead flame of my father's? My mother never found out, but, at my christening, my godmother's name, Geraldine, was quietly slipped in instead. My father and mother obviously had a great many secrets from each other.

It would have broken my mother's heart if she had not had a son. It was whispered that Elisabeth Marshall, my father's mistress, had already borne him two sons (the first called Ralph, after him), each sturdy and good-looking. How ironic that my poor mother should behave so unsatisfactorily!

All was forgiven, one warm day in July 1902, when our own Henry John Ralph was born. Daphne and I, aged four and eighteen months, were hastily packed off to Lord and Lady Digby's at Minterne to be out of the way. The great bell in the stables at Kingston Lacy resounded at the moment of birth and wild celebrations began. Oxen were roasted whole, bonfires lit, fireworks exploded into the balmy air. Excitement and relief flooded house, farm and estate, at the long-awaited leap into life of my curly haired, baby brother.

Though Daphne and I were the sole occupants of the large nursery on the top floor of Kingston Lacy for a few years, it is impossible to think of it now without Ralph. My first memory of him is of a tiny, round doll with a few wisps of curly fair hair, in his short, white dress with narrow lace frill, dumped unceremoniously on the thick patterned carpet for us to play with. Interrupted in an interesting game, we stared rather glumly at him, not appreciating our special treat very much. He stared wordlessly back with serious, china-blue eyes. We tried to increase his entertainment value by poking and prodding him a little, and making an observation about his 'little tassel'. However, a scandalised nurse burst in and, with loud scolding, plucked him indignantly away.

We watched him grow out of the domineering vulnerability of babyhood, when he was cosseted, pampered and protected, into a self-sufficient, strong little toddler, solid and very masculine, despite his golden curls. He would usually sit in a corner, deaf to any of our remarks, totally absorbed in the nursery problem of fitting wooden shapes together with his chubby hands or building swaying towers of gaudy red and yellow blocks. I would probably be violently creaking up and down on the huge, dappled rocking horse, inspired by its red flaring nostrils, bared teeth and wicked eye to wild adventures in story-book lands, or kneeling beside the dolls' house my father had given me, looking with its pink and white bricks like the tall seventeenth-century Dutch houses in Pieter de Hoogh's pictures; rearranging the miniature furniture, rehanging the round silver paper mirror or fluffing up the tiny pink eiderdown on the bed. Daphne might be placidly embroidering a violet in the corner of a white cotton square, in huge, vivid stitches, occasionally stopping to flick her long, shining hair over her shoulder, listening to the singing of the canary.

My favourite soft toys were a black golliwog with blue

coat, brass buttons and scarlet trousers and a smiling, turned-up mouth, and a plump stuffed dog called Leo which I used to drag along for walks up and down the long nursery on a leather string. I also had a pink-cheeked doll in cotton dress and 'undies' with head, neck and hands of wax and blue staring eyes. I loved combing her 'real' yellow hair and curling it, using tiny curling tongs, just like my mother's full-sized ones, which rested in a long narrow iron stand with a hollow in the middle, on four feet. I was always anxiously warned not to burn myself, or Daphne, as I heated the tongs over a miniature spirit lamp.

Our first nanny ('Nurse' to my mother and the servants), who was so shocked at our not knowing how to play with our new baby brother, was Nanny Turrell. She had transferred to Ralph from the infant future Lord Portarlington. Years later, when my husband and I had moved our family from the wartime dangers of London to the comparative safety of South Ascot, I would regularly meet his stout, grown-up, aimiable lordship, by then handicapped, miraculously speeding down the leafy lane in his new-fangled, electric wheelchair.

'How d'y' do?' he would ask in his beautifully modulated public school voice, always pleased to see me. It was a great bond to have had a nanny in common, but our hazy infant memories would not allow any Nanny Turrell reminiscences.

Nanny slept in Ralph's bright and airy room next to ours, in the nursery suite. The nursery maids took care of Daphne and me. My special favourite was Alice Maud Baker, willowy, delicate-looking, and gentle.

'Alice Maud Baker!' we would shout imperiously, in our shrill little voices, taking her patient kindness for granted when we wanted her to get down on her hands and knees on the nursery floor and play with us.

Daphne and I would wake up together in the chilly morning, in the unheated room and peer through the white hoop rails at the end of our beds to see Alice blacking the grate of the huge stone fireplace, laying the fire with paper, sticks, coal and logs, lighting it and fanning it with the brass and leather bellows. She would already have made the fires in two or three other cold bedrooms, having risen at four thirty, in her own, cheerless room under the slate roof.

As the fire blazed up, she would lean with both arms on the guard, in her white apron over a blue cotton dress with a white collar, her soft fair hair curling under the edges of her little white bonnet, gazing sadly into the flames that crackled round the logs, sweet-smelling beech, elm and oak, dry from having been carefully stored winter after winter. Had she been right to leave her cosy family for the Spartan life of service in a Stately Home? It never occurred to anyone to wonder if she was well or happy. A few years later, her sorrowing parents complained bitterly when, taken to hospital much too late for a successful appendectomy, quietly and uncomplainingly, she died.

'Come on, Miss Daphne and Miss Cissie,' (I was always called 'Cissie' at home until I was thirteen) 'get out of bed!' Once out of bed, we would stand in front of the fire while she dressed us in the clothes she had hung on the guard to warm.

We always wore Jaeger combinations in soft, creamy-grey wool, 'wool next to the skin' being an inflexible rule in those days. They had short sleeves and came down to our knees. Under our petticoats we also wore cotton knickers made at home and long black stockings, like little nuns. Parisian, flesh-coloured stockings did not come in till 1912. Our black shoes were fastened tightly by a strap with one button. At first our frocks and pinafores were white which was then thought a very hygienic colour for children, as it showed the dirt. When I was four, white changed to grey. For some strange, then unexplained reason, we were in mourning.

The nurserymaid brushed and coaxed my hair into its long ringlets. Daphne's was fair, fine, fly-away, mine more wiry and dark brown with golden ends. Neither head of hair had any natural curl at all, so that after a day outside, it would always hang straight as a ruler. Nor did Mama encourage any extravagant decoration. One nurserymaid, who had paid to take hairdressing lessons in Wimborne, once led me down to the saloon to be shown off to my mother's guests wearing a huge, white ribbon bow. Mama's hand immediately shot out to flatten down the beautiful butterfly.

After making us presentable, Alice would look in the mirror herself, straightening her bonnet and pinning back a stray curl before appearing before Nanny in the Day Nursery for breakfast.

Breakfast cereals had not been invented then. We ate toast and eggs and bacon or smoked haddock, and there was always a quarter of a honeycomb oozing with the pale lavender-scented honey that came from the buzzing hive in the kitchen garden, next to the great lavender hedge. We drank fresh milk from the Home Farm from shining, silver Christening mugs, mine given to me by my formidable Dorset godmother, Lady Glyn. Her husband, Sir Richard, an old gentleman with white hair and white moustache, who sometimes came to tea with us, had been in the Charge of the Light Brigade. We always behaved very well at meals, having both the nurse and the nurserymaid to train us in nursery etiquette, not letting us put our elbows on the table or make too many crumbs. No cooking was ever done on the nursery and schoolroom floor, though Nanny used to make tea on a little meths stove with three claws which held a saucepan.

The Day Nursery was a large, cheerful room with an attractive wallpaper of blue ribbons entwined with small bunches of horizontally arranged roses. It always had a roaring fire on which burned huge logs and coal brought up four flights of stairs by the 'Odd Man'. There was a large, oval William and Mary mirror, bordered by swirling arabesques painted in greenish-grey paint. We used to preen ourselves or pull monstrous faces in front of it. The only sign that other children had been brought up there was a three-piece screen which my own father, when a little boy, had covered in colourful Victorian scraps. The tall, old-fashioned windows, unobstructed by bars, were always kept closed when we were likely to look out, so that we could not fall through while peering at the view, and plunge to our deaths on the tidy gravel paths below.

On one side, over the Italian terrace, we could see the level, green lawn, three centuries old, meticulously mown by two gardeners, Charlie Hart who could not read or write but put a cross when asked to sign a document, and Fred Ivimey, who became bowed and delicate from bending down so much to pull out the weeds. The mower was horse-drawn, the horse wearing huge leather over-shoes to stop its hooves sinking into the lawn. The turf was protected from burrowing rabbits and moles by the game-keeper's ruthless ferreting and trapping, any impertinent mounds being raked out with a harrow.

Right in the middle of the lawn was the pink granite obelisk, sister to Cleopatra's Needle. It had been unearthed from the Egyptian sands at Philae, in 1815, by my roving great uncle, William John Bankes, Lord Byron's friend, and had taken fourteen years to reach our Dorset garden. The obelisk was dedicated to Osiris, Amun and Isis. On the base in Greek, and higher up, in hieroglyphic cartouches or elongated oval shapes, were the inscriptions, 'Cleopatra' and 'Ptolemy, living for ever, beloved of Ptah.'

Just as Cleopatra's Needle had come adrift in its cast iron container and been abandoned for months in the Bay of Biscay, so the Kingston Lacy obelisk had wickedly slipped into the muddy waters of the River Nile and defied many attempts to rescue it. Having finally reached Kingston Lacy it seemed totally satisfied to lie recumbent on the grass, and it took nineteen horses to drag it up into position. The Duke of Wellington, another illustrious friend of William John, laid its foundation stone. King George IV gave its pink granite pedestal which was so convenient for jumping on and off in our garden games. Equally useful as a base was the pink granite Egyptian mummy which also lay on the lawn, until my mother took a dislike to it and had it removed.

When I was a child I was fascinated to know that, in the Egyptian Royal family, brother and sister could marry and rule together. I could make out the ancient markings on the obelisk very clearly and was told that they were of as much historical value as the Rosetta Stone which had been found in Egypt in 1799 and was the first clue to deciphering hieroglyphics. The British weather was already whittling away at the inscriptions — a fact deeply depressing to my mother, who felt a personal responsibility for the monument. She would willingly have had it entirely encased in a gigantic glass cover, if anyone could have thought of a way of stopping the glass from cracking in the frost.

Beyond the obelisk was the ha-ha, a six-foot drop down a

stone wall to a wet ditch at the bottom, separating the lawn
from the pasture where the sheep grazed. It foiled us children as well as the animals, though it would have made a
very good hiding place if we could ever have climbed out of
it again. Beyond the ha-ha was the Park with the Blandford
and Wimborne Drives. We would kneel on the low window
seats, pressing our noses to the glass and watch people
coming and going. There were all kinds of horse-drawn
vehicles: Victorias; smaller, one horse, closed carriages,
called after Lord Brougham; pony-chaises just for one or
two people; little round pony-carts; and the humble wagonettes which always carried people's luggage up from the
station to the house even after my mother had bought a car.

We could watch, on the other side of the lawn, the puppet-
sized figures of my mother's married or clerical friends
sedately playing tennis, or gaze over the grass court to the
meadows beyond, shaded by the stately cedars. There were
two handsome, smooth leaved, dark green mulberry trees,
higher than oaks but not as high as beeches, whose juicy,
dark purple fruit used simply to drop down onto the ground
ready to be made into mulberry jam. Mulberry trees had
come to England in the reign of James I and were very
fashionable in Charles II's time when Kingston Lacy was
built. As is always said to happen, when one mulberry tree
died, the other sickened and died in sympathy.

Each happy nursery morning ended with a plentiful
lunch, cold boiled bacon with hot vegetables being Nanny's
favourite dish. The thick, red cloth on the table, on which
we rested our paintings or pushed our model cars and
trains along, would be covered over by a crisp, starched
white one. Once more the cheerful, beaming 'Odd Man'
would climb the four flights of stairs to the nursery with
our meal on an outsize black japanned tray with a flowered

pattern, the food kept at just the right heat by a tin tray of hot water fitted under the bottom of each plate.

After our afternoon rest, when we lay on our backs, we always went for a walk. Children were never expected to do anything for themselves, in those days, if they had maids. So we would stretch out our legs for Alice or Winnie to fasten the hooks on our high button boots, then, weather permitting, we would set off, with the Nurse and the nurserymaid in their grey coats, nurserymaid pushing the pram, Nanny walking majestically behind. We went across the lawn, along the Ladies' Walk through the wood, carpeted with snowdrops, primroses, bluebells or lilies of the valley, depending on the season; down the lane; past the farm, perhaps calling at the post office in the thatched cottage, and back home up the Wimborne Drive. Ralph at first travelled in state in his high pram, Daphne and I dawdling behind to pick flowers. Fortunately, the 'century of the child' having begun, we were dressed, for every day, not in the latest grown-up fashion, but simply and with complete freedom of movement, in grey pullovers, probably knitted at home, full, straight grey serge skirts and grey serge caps like the workmen wore.

It was no wonder that we were rather buxom children, considering the voracious appetites the fresh country air invariably gave us. We ate as much as we wanted for supper; usually a fish course, followed by a milky pudding then apples or pears or luscious green figs from the mountain of fresh Kingston Lacy fruit always set before us in an old green Staffordshire dish.

Sometimes, our mother would come and read to us while we ate, often, *King Solomon's Mines* by Rider Haggard, because she knew his brother, the diplomat Sir William Haggard. These sessions, though enjoyable, could be very nerve-wracking. On one occasion, I inadvisedly interrupted her reading of *The Violet Fairy Book* with a remark which I fondly hoped she would think very intelligent. She turned on me a face of stone and frigidly commanded me to keep quiet. Bitterly disappointed by this unexpected humiliation, I burst into noisy tears, which irritated her still more.

In my teenage years, in similar situations, I was much more likely to develop a painful stitch from desperately trying to control my irrepressible, nervous giggles. Ralph would calmly go on eating, without seeming to notice that anything had happened, while Daphne, if not suddenly afflicted with a great rush of hysterical giggles herself, would smile at me sympathetically.

Daphne and I had a Queen Anne dressing table in our room, whose dark, wooden top would lift up to reveal a space for our white wooden hairbrushes and tortoiseshell combs. There was no bathroom at Kingston Lacy, until our mother put in a very plain one later on. For ordinary washing, a man-servant carried up a huge can of hot water for the large white jug and basin in our room. At bathtime, a zinc hip bath, high at the back, low at the front, would be put down on the cold linoleum in front of the bedroom fire. Alice or Winnie, another nurserymaid, armed with coal tar soap for us to use, would check that the water was just the right temperature and then pour it over us as we rubbed and scrubbed ourselves. When we were out of the bath and snugly swathed in the huge, soft, white towels which had been warming before the fire on the towel horse, a man-servant, tactfully averting his eyes, would take the bath away.

In summer, when the whole household moved to the Manor House at Studland Bay, the zinc bath would travel there too. It would be packed with the mountain of suitcases in the largest farm waggon, drawn by two enormously powerful, good-tempered, chestnut-coloured Suffolk Punch horses from the farm, and greeted with gleeful shouts of recognition when we overtook it with difficulty by car, in the narrow, winding Dorset lanes.

At bedtime, the nurserymaids would gently brush our long hair and, in my case, begin the interminable preparation of the next day's ringlets. We would sit in front of the fire, trying not to wriggle, in our flannel dressing gowns, mine scarlet, treasured and much let down, and Daphne's a bright emerald green. The shadows of the maids' busy hands danced jerkily over the walls in the candlelight as they chatted and joked, one twisting each recalcitrant lock of mine into curling rags which felt just like stones when I later laid my head on the pillow.

'Sleep well, Miss,' they said to each of us, as they tucked us in, and left us to say our prayers by ourselves if we wanted to.

Tucked under our beds were the 'vases de nuit', vitally necessary, since we would never have dared to venture out into the dark oak passage, once the candles had gone out. Sadly, our 'members', as we called them, did not bear a Coat of Arms as did those in another house which we sometimes visited.

At Kingston Lacy, as the fire sank to a lifeless glow, our short, fat night lights flickered and danced in their white saucers on the bedside tables. We would wake to a chorus of birdsong through the open windows, from the rhododendrons and the meadows at the back of the house and the tall cedars and mulberries at the front. After the last 'Goodnight and goodmorrow' hoot of an owl came the strident call of pheasants, the soft, coaxing coo of pigeons and twittering of sparrows, starlings and finches. There were jays, too, in the wood, but these the keeper shot as, he said,

'Them birds are mischievious.'

One day a shadow fell over this comfortable life. Nanny Turrell passed onto the next new-born baby and into our happy nursery routine stepped the heavy-handed, tall, grim personage of Nurse Stanley. Her dark gimlet eyes, set close together in her long, red face above her thin pointed nose, offered no hope of any affection. Where on earth did our mother find her, she who was usually so careful about references? Her hair was scraped up on top, secured by a savage tortoise-shell pin. Beneath her white apron, stiff as card, were visible black skirt, thin black stockinged bony legs, ankles, and flat black, thick laced shoes. Perhaps her unattractiveness had seemed a guarantee of reliability? Not even her grating voice, hard Cockney accent and coarse attitudes were sufficient warning for our innocent mother.

'How dare you upset Master Ralph! Go to bed at once, Miss Cissie'.

'Miss Daphne, you wicked girl! There'll be no home-made bread and honey for you today.'

Life seemed, all of a sudden, to have turned into a series of deprivations. Her one aim was apparently to make us miserable. I suppose all children had their fingers painted with bitter aloes when they gnawed their nails, but Nurse Stanley revelled in giving us the purgative powder, un-doing the little paper wrapper with great relish. It was probably true, too, that sweets would have been bad for our teeth, but Nanny took an unnatural delight in banning them. We did not have iced cakes, except for birthdays, but we loved as a special treat, to have caster sugar sprinkled on our homebaked, crusty white bread.

'No sugar today!' she would say, 'You've been very naughty.' Then I would probably hit my little brother or pull Daphne's long fair hair.

Poor Alice was scolded from breakfast to bedtime for being too slow and often stood weeping silently while Nurse Stanley went through a list of her shortcomings and threatened her with ignominious dismissal. 'And don't you think you'll ever get another post when you've lost this one!'

Even our Mama was cowed into submission. 'Yes, Nanny. No, Nanny. I'm quite sure you're right, Nanny.' There would have been absolutely no point in complaining to her. When our mother came upstairs, we were always quiet and everything seemed to be in order in the nursery. Nanny Stanley reigned supreme. Then Ralph, who had always been so irritatingly uncommunicative, suddenly began to bellow and roar. Contented grunts or absorbed silences changed to a continuous wail of bitter frustration which drove Daphne and me as far away from him as possible.

'Thank goodness for Nanny!' thought our hopelessly inexperienced mother.

I hated to see Ralph, no longer healthy, but increasingly pale and sickly, beating on his high chair with his spoon and turning his head away while Nanny Stanley forced more and more sinister dark red liquid into his screaming mouth. The weaker he became, so she must have thought, the more my poor mother would depend upon her. In winter, when all three of us had coughs, colds and catarrh, Nurse Stanley used to sit poor, wheezing Ralph beside her in the ponycart to go to terrorize the shopkeepers in Wimborne, none of whom dared to offend her for fear of losing Kingston Lacy's custom. An indignant tradesman, much braver than the rest, wrote to my mother:

'Dear Madam,

I take the liberty to write and tell you that the little

squire looked frozen as your nurse sat in the open ponycart for quarter of an hour with a howling wind. I think it
is very bad for a young child to have to undergo this.'
My mother was grateful, yet even this incident did not
completely shake her trust in Nanny.

If we had only realised it, Daphne and I had a secret
weapon. We knew that Nurse Stanley was subject to fits.
Once, finding the door of the night nursery locked, I had
wrestled with the handle and heard strange muffled sounds
coming from inside. It became commonplace for Nanny,
feeling an attack coming on, to disappear while a nurserymaid quietly took over. Little Jinky, the cook-housekeeper,
realised that Nanny had epilepsy, for which at the time
there was no effective treatment, but no servant at Kingston Lacy would ever tell upon another.

Nanny Stanley's disagreeable behaviour became more
and more oppressive. Probably listening at the key hole, if
she heard the slightest whisper from Daphne or me after
'lights out', she would fling open the door and say,
'You've been talking! Turn over!', seizing the oportunity
to smack our little bottoms. One day, when I cried as she
roughly brushed the tangles out of my hair, she said cross-
ly, 'I shan't give you the whole of the birthday present I
promised you. I shall only give you half.' It had been going
to be a box of writing paper and a medallion enamelled
with the charmingly sentimental portrait of a pretty little
girl by the eighteenth century artist, Jean Baptiste Greuze.
She kept the medallion.

Nurse Stanley also became more and more insolent to
our mother. Once, when Mama had been away to London,
she returned to find that Nanny had cut all Ralph's precious
curls off. Another time, when she had bought her son and
heir (she never brought Daphne and me any toys, of course)

a present, she was very badly hurt by Nanny's attitude. It was a large, wooden box containing a gleaming battalion of little lead infantrymen in scarlet tunics and black busbies, and Daphne and I held our breath, experiencing the pleasure at second hand, as Ralph stretched out to take it.

'Oh, no! You mustn't have those!' interposed Nurse Stanley. She seized the box and confiscated it. My poor mother, though very distressed, still let Nanny have her way.

Perhaps we would have suffered indefinitely from Nanny's cruelty, if Ralph's condition had not deteriorated so alarmingly that our mother at last began to wonder if Nanny really did know best. He had terrifying spasms of crying and developed eccentric mannerisms. He would blow out his nostrils like the fiery rocking horse or open his mouth very wide as though he was going to yawn, then shut it again. Finally, most frightening of all, his eyes became so sensitive that he could hardly keep them open. A London specialist was summoned.

He found, to his fury, that the drink Nanny Stanley had forced Ralph to swallow, the juice of one pound of raw beef, was the only daily food she had allowed him. In trying to keep him weak and dependent on her, she had almost killed him.

To the great relief of Daphne and me, Nurse Stanley suddenly vanished, smuggled out of the nursery and into a Home by Canon Sowter, a friend who was to play an increasing part in our lives. There, guilt and remorse, coupled with epilepsy, drove her out of her mind.

Sanity returned to our nursery in the shape of efficient, brisk Nurse Startin. Director of her own nursing home in Bournemouth and not very keen to leave it, she took pity on my desperate mother and came to stay at Kingston Lacy, coaxing Ralph back to health with real food and putting drops into his eyes every day, until they grew strong again. My mother once more began to smile and was so grateful to Nurse Startin, or 'Little Connie', that she gave her a reproduction of Raphael's *Sistine Madonna*. Raphael's Christ Child looks very stalwart, healthy and well-cared for, in true Nurse Startin fashion.

After Nurse Startin came a long train of blue-veiled hospital nurses to look after Ralph, and cast an occasional eye upon Daphne and me. Ralph, the little squire, was so pampered and spoilt that, I am sorry to say, Daphne and I did not feel protective or motherly towards him as older sisters like to do. We ignored him, as he pedalled his red and green toy car round and round the nursery floor or up and down the corridors, banging into anyone who happened to be coming along.

Soon, however, nursery days were over and it was time for new, exciting territory – the school room.

3
Governesses

'Will Daddy be home for Christmas, I wonder?' I speculated idly one morning at breakfast, when I was nine years old.

'Don't be silly, Cissie! How can you talk like that when you know that your father is dead?'

With this stark presentation of the truth by our unthinking governess, cold reality broke into our world.

It was a totally absent-minded mistake and our horrified and hysterical reaction must have frightened and upset her. Nobody had ever told us anything unpleasant before. Children were supposed to live in a state of blissful innocence. One day, when I had run down to the stables to find my sheepdog puppy, he had not been waiting for me, as usual. Nobody, not even the kind old coachman, would tell me where he was. Eventually, a young groom, crouching down rubbing at a horse's leg, realising that I would never stop cross-examining him until I found out the truth, muttered through his teeth:

'You'll never see him again, Miss.'

He never told me what had happened to the puppy. Similarly, it never occurred to anyone that Daphne, Ralph or I should be told about our father's death. We had obediently gone into mourning without having the slightest idea why.

Knowing himself to be dying of heart-disease, my father had joined in a conspiracy to deceive us. He was going to India, he said, to collect cowrie shells which were very valuable. When he had enough, he would buy us a boat.

Although we did not know it, he had never left the house

again, retiring for ever to his huge, dark oak, four-poster bed. His room, which was two lonely flights of white marble stairs below my mother's, had been decorated by nineteenth-century Italian workmen imported by William John. It was painted with arabesques of flowers, birds and animals, called 'Grotteschi', after similar paintings on grottoes in Italian gardens and on the indoor shutters of Italian galleries and villas.

In a house as massive as Kingston Lacy, particularly when we children used only the back stairs and were never allowed to approach the marble staircase, it was easy to keep the presence of an invalid a secret. We did not know that one day, the black-veiled figure of his mistress slipped into the house to say goodbye; that, as he grew weaker, perhaps partly owing to the leeches which covered his body, he became an increasingly difficult patient; that, eventually, grasping for life in a final moment of panic, he had seized his male nurse by the throat, almost strangling him, before dropping back, dead, onto his bed.

We three had still gone on waiting for him to return from India. Every summer, we had faithfully padded bare-foot over the silver sands at Studland, eyes on the ground, searching for cowrie shells for him. We had asked the nurse and the servants about him now and again, but had always received carefully evasive replies.

To suddenly hear that he had been dead for five years was a shocking experience.

It was our lost idea of him that we mourned. I also wept long and bitterly at the mockery of the non-existent boat we had all dreamed about for so long.

Children forget very quickly and our father's death did not overshadow us for long. After all, at Kingston Lacy, people were always coming and going. We saw our mother every day and could always speak to her when we wanted to, though she was also busy running the estate. It was not our parents, but our governesses on whom our happiness most depended.

Our mother, eager for us to be educated for our roles in Society, saw to it that we had governesses of almost every European nationality. First, there was Miss Thomas, a vibrant, quick-speaking Welsh woman, who rouged (which in those days was a very '*défendu*' thing to do) and wore a wig with hair piled up high on top and a golden brown fringe, in imitation of Queen Alexandra. Very neat by nature, the only lesson I remember learning from her was how not to appear in public. Even when I was nine it seemed outrageous to me that she dared come to meals with my stately mother with unsightly white ointment dabbed on the many spots on her fiery red cheeks. I wonder if she removed it when Royalty came to lunch? She was soon banished from Kingston Lacy.

The school room was large and light and looked out over the park. Through the open windows would come the lowing of the Red Devon cows that sometimes mooed and called for three days at a time, mourning their calves which had been sold for veal.

We had very comfortable William and Mary cane chairs with grey and white painted woodwork, whose wide seats would have suited the widest crinolines or earlier Lely dresses. We children used to tip backwards and forwards on them with scant regard for their antique value.

Daphne and I were usually the only pupils in the large school room. When Ralph was tiny he stayed in the nursery, then, later, he went to a dame school in Bournemouth. At home, he was never an ideal student, always lazy and reluctant to learn. He was allowed to do exactly as he wished, wandering off to his carpentry or playing stolidly with his Meccano if he did not feel like lessons. Daphne and I worked hard. All the same, we were a little incredulous when, closely questioned about some parcels she had put on the table, our one English governess, Miss Tidmarsh, said, very primly, 'They are prizes.'

I had 'won', for German, a little bee clock, which in those days cost five shillings. It kept perfect time and I was delighted, even if I secretly sensed that to be first out of two, in one subject, could not be the pinnacle of academic achievement.

Daphne and I had a lively, if superficial interest in the wide variety of subjects on which strict, middle-aged Miss Tidmarsh was a sound authority. She had come to us from Lady Dimsdale, wife of a Lord Mayor of London and had had a totally unblemished career until she eventually blotted it with us. She was very trim with a tiny waist and frizzed up hair, quite pretty except for the forbidding *pince-nez* that perched on her nose. She sat up as straight as a pillar and was continually telling us to do the same.

During the reign of Miss Tidmarsh, the Arts flourished in the school room of Kingston Lacy. She played Dvořák or other pieces every night on the piano and I became quite proficient myself – a dangerous accomplishment which I lived to regret later, in my débutante days, when I was pressed by my host, Walter Batten-Poole, into playing in the interval before lunch at his country house party. Much was expected of someone who had had so many governesses! In my shyness, I played on and on, not hearing the quiet announcement that luncheon was ready, while the bored and hungry guests waited interminably for me to finish.

We also recited poetry for Miss Tidmarsh, standing up in the schoolroom and declaiming *The Arab's Farewell to His Horse* by Caroline Norton.

'My beautiful, my beautiful, that standest meekly by,
With thy proudly arched and glossy neck
And dark and fiery eye.'

At the lines:

'Free not to roam the desert more
My beautiful, thou'rt sold,'

I used to pretend that I had forgotten the rest. I could not say it without weeping and never reached the happy ending, where the Arab changes his mind, jumps on his steed and gallops away.

Ralph's dame school, Wychwood, run by dear, tall, toothy Miss Maddox, from which he returned each weekend by car, did not fill him with an equally passionate love for words. He appeared one holiday with an impressive, leather bound edition of *Ivanhoe*.

'Are you going to read all that, Boysie?' we asked, with respect.

'No, too much fag!' he replied.

On clear nights, Miss Tidmarsh would lead Daphne and me round to different windows to stare up at the heavens. We would forget that we were safe on the top floor of Kingston Lacy and imagine that we were three intrepid explorers out on a wide sea, with no compass to steer by. She taught us to identify bright Orion, the Hunter, with his sword and belt and showed us the constellation of the Plough pointing the way to the Pole Star.

On warm, spring days, we would poke about with her in Cowgrove Pond, getting satisfactorily muddy as we scooped up fat, slippery black tadpoles which we would keep in a jar to stare at and study in the school room until they turned into tiny, jumping frogs. They had to be hastily returned to their own reedy world when they began to take a springy interest in their lofty, educational environment.

Sometimes, we would painstakingly dissect a flower under Miss Tidmarsh's direction, examining stamens, pistils or bulging green seedbox, or make collections of wild flowers, meticulously labelling their delicate forms in simple, picturesque vernacular and more pompous Latin: buttercup ... *ranunculus bubosus*; daisy ... *bellis perennis*; harebell ... *campanula rotundifolia* – a very heavy-sounding name for the delicately drooping blue flower which swayed and trembled in the slightest breeze.

The only biological facts about which the knowledgeable Miss Tidmarsh would suddenly become unaccountably vague were those which we would have found most enthralling.

'Oh, Miss Tidmarsh, do look at those cows! Why is one jumping on the other?' we would urgently ask.

'Oh, dear, I don't know at all,' she would answer, suddenly increasing the pace of our nature ramble, drawing us hastily away from the interesting Red Devons.

'Come along! Don't dawdle!'

'I shouldn't do that, dear, if I were you,' she would say when I suggested I might ask my mother about it.

The trouble with governesses was that you could never escape them. They were always with you, unless you could occasionally slip away up past the maids' cold rooms onto the forbidden roof. Being naughty in lessons always led to reprisals in the rest of your life. It was bad enough being made to stand in the corner with your face to the wall, totally humiliated if the manservant came in with a bucket of coal. Even more annoying was the fact that you could not leave your school self behind at the end of the day, as most children do, but had to carry it with you till bedtime, which could be advanced by several hours to make up for some satisfying but shortlived insurrection, or some unintentional accident, such as upsetting a vase of wild flowers over Miss Tidmarsh's neat pile of books.

I did not terribly mind going to bed while it was still light. My bedroom was one of two at Kingston Lacy which had been decorated to look like tents, in order, it was said, to please Ernest Augustus, Duke of Cumberland, brother to George IV and later King of Hanover. In 1803, he had become the commanding military officer of the South Western District of Hampshire, Dorset and Wiltshire, and would have been a frequent visitor at Kingston Lacy.

The room was painted with broad white and blue stripes and red wooden tassels, though army tents in Ernest Augustus's day had been made of plain white canvas. Blue and white striped tents may have been made for some Royal occasion of which no record exists – George III's bathing machine, still preserved at Weymouth, was, after all, coloured blue and white. Whatever the truth of the matter, our mother did not like my 'tent', thinking it grim and dark. She had it repapered with a pattern of large roses.

I enjoyed lying in bed looking at my Goss china models from places we had visited, such as Salisbury, Bath and Wells or Cheddar Gorge, on the three-shelf book case. There was also a picture called *Sweetest Eyes Were Ever Seen* of a pretty girl in a black lace bonnet painted by Herbert Schmatz who hastily changed his name to Herbert Carmichael during the 1914-18 war. Another coloured print comforted me in my isolation. It was of a girl sitting with a pile of books, entitled *A Good Book is the Best Companion*.

What did hurt about my banishments was being sent to bed without tea of bread and plum jam, and then not being allowed to get up for supper either.

On one embarrasing day, we were summoned downstairs by my mother to be given a present by Mr. Ponting. Ponting was a soft-voiced, pale-skinned architect whose eyes twinkled through his gold-rimmed spectacles as he smilingly watched us playing. He often stayed at Kingston Lacy, where there was always building going on, and was given caramel pudding whenever he did so because he had once, unguardedly, said he liked it.

That afternoon, he had brought two gold lockets, surrounded by pearls on a gold background: one for me, containing a picture of Ralph painted on ivory; the other for Daphne, with a portrait of our mother inside it.

'I have had to send Cissie to bed.' said Miss Tidmarsh, which rather spoilt the charm of the occasion.

No wonder that we sometimes teased Miss Tidmarsh, even though we respected her, and took a mischievous delight in hiding from her. Once we had gone to roost in the loft when important guests were being shown round the stables below. The disembodied voices of children mysteriously seeming to come from horses did not amuse my mother. She sternly held Miss Tidmarsh responsible.

Poor Miss Tidmarsh eventually disappeared intothe void. Unforgiveably, as far as my mother was concerned, she had squeezed herself, in a hat covered with huge cabbage roses, into the family group as it was being photographed with the Kaiser on the terrace. Moreover she took away with her his signatures on Kingston Lacy notepaper, which he had given to Daphne and me during his visit. A few years afterwards, a Mrs Jefferson, a society beauty in King Edwards VII's time, came across the signatures at a charity bazaar in Berkeley Square, bought them and triumphantly returned them to my mother.

Miss Tidmarsh had certainly been more dynamic than Mademoiselle Berger who followed her. Our critical school girl eyes noted that where Miss Tidmarsh was trim and even stylish in her long skirts, Mademoiselle Berger was inclined to bulge. In her case, *pince-nez* were not enough to suggest the necessary strictness to keep three boisterous children in order. Her mouth was always ready to tremble and her pale eyes to fill with tears when Ralph made no secret of his contempt for French, or when, bored with teasing her, he would wander rudely away from her ineffectual attempts to interest him. Daphne and I were not on her side either, not being totally charmed by her habit of comparing us unfavourably with 'dear Mida and Sybil', the children of the Duke of Buccleuch with whom she had been before.

A later French governess, Madame Scottie, red-haired and statuesque, was a strangely sophisticated companion for children.

'Mon Dieu, que cette histoire est bête!' she would exclaim, yawning ostentatiously and breaking off from her rendering of one of our cherished Charles Perrault fairy stories, as we lay on our backs after lunch.

We had German and Italian governesses, the latter a Roman Catholic, trying unsuccessfully to persuade us to say the Lord's prayer in Latin. We resolutely refused to learn more than a few words of German or Italian. Many visiting teachers over the years were collected from Wimborne Station by the coachman in the dogcart, all women, until, when we were thirteen or fourteen, a seedy, pompous gentleman arrived to teach us Greek. He would put his top hat upside down on the ground beside us before he began. Acting as a chaperon, the butler would always interrupt his lessons in the middle with milk and biscuits. I cannot remember learning a single line of Greek. In Summer we were taught sketching outside, sitting under an old Irish yew tree with a flaking trunk. In Miss Tidmarsh's day, art and other much resented afternoon lessons took place, on hot days, under a lime tree, to which the footman would carry the heavily laden silver tray at five o'clock, through the dining room and down the steps on the terrace.

Our last governess was Miss Vyfhuis, English, but of Dutch extraction, niece of Mr Ponting. She came from Barbados which, she said, had an 'even' climate and whose colourful stamps from her relations' letters she gave us for our albums. We liked her on sight and excitedly dragged her off to see the garden and the farm, making our mother, who had thought we were going out with her, very jealous. To be successful a governess must keep her popularity under control.

4
Out of doors

When in 1981, the National Trust accepted my brother's bequest of Kingston Lacy, it was impossible not to regret that it would no longer remain in the family, yet this was the only way to keep it intact. The roof of the house needed releading; the dry rot was so serious that you could look down into one of the ground floor rooms from the bedroom; the greenish Chilmark stone, with which, between 1835 and 1839, Sir Charles Barry had refaced Roger Pratt's seventeenth-century brick building, was being exploded by the rusting iron cramps. Even the thirteen acre garden was semi-derelict. No single family could ever afford the cost of restoration. By his decisive action, my brother had ensured that our beautiful home, its pictures, books, and treasures, for which my mother had sacrificed her whole widowhood, until his majority, would be preserved for ever.

Mama had not taken very naturally to being the wife of an English squire. When she had first met my father she had been overwhelmed by his elegant charm. Once the marriage was signed and sealed and her fate decided for ever, she discovered that he was perhaps not quite as exciting as she had thought. After safely capturing his beautiful bride, he had returned to his country pleasures: hunting, shooting, fishing and racing, drinking a bottle of port a day, not bothering to talk very much to anyone, except the gamekeeper and, perhaps, his secret mistress.

His conversation began to bore my mother, even in the

earliest days of their marriage, when they spent more time in their London home in Wilton Crescent than at Kingston Lacy.

'Why doesn't he go to his Club?' she would ask wearily, when he relentlessly reappeared for lunch, 'I never heard of a husband coming home to lunch everyday'.

In the country, his taciturnity deepened. Coming downstairs one morning, my mother found a terse note from him: 'Have gone to New York.'

Notes were his only form of comunication with the servants and, even when he was alive, my mother, with her deep sense of duty, must have taken on most of the responsibility of house and estate. After his early death, apart from visits to London in the season, or to fashionable European Spas for 'cures', she devoted herself to the estate entirely, determined that it should be passed on, thriving and prosperous, to Ralph.

So it was that the life of the house busily continued, floors shining, furniture lovingly cared for, the leather of the chairs in the library where my mother worked, so grey and brittle when the National Trust took over, kept supple and glowing a warm red. On the Kingston Lacy and Corfe Castle estate, the two hundred and fifty or so farm houses and cottages were maintained and new ones built. Many of the old families who had lived in the same villages for generations still do: the Framptons, Crabbs and Jewells at Shapwick; the Kerleys and Ricketts at Cowgrove and Pamphill and the Stockleys in enormous numbers in Corfe Castle village.

My mother and the estate agent, Alfred Lodder, watched over them all, making sure that all complaints were dealt with, roofs rethatched where necessary, and leaks stopped. many of the cottages were very old, with little drainage and probably no plumbing at all, though money was plentiful and building never stopped. Usually, Mr Lodder would say, 'A five pun' note would meet the case.'

The oldest tenant farmer on the Bankes estate was Mr Joyce who made the tenants' speech at the reception at Kingston Lacy when my father brought my mother there as his bride. My grandfather later offered Mr Joyce the freehold of his farm, 'White Mill,' because of the long association of his family with the Bankes family, but the proud old man refused it, saying, 'Thank you, but a Joyce always pays for what he has.'

The park and the garden were meticulously tended. To Daphne, Ralph and me, not even realising how lucky we were, as long as we obeyed the rules, it was a perfectly ordered Paradise. We could go anywhere we liked but, for example, were not allowed to pick the peaches or the grapes which the head gardener, Mr Hill, was preparing for the local horticultural show. With ten gardeners in winter and twenty in summer, some of whom worked only in the hot houses, it was no wonder that the local people began to object to my mother's flowers, fruit and vegetables continually carrying off the prizes. In the end, their resentment reached such unpleasant proportions that she had to stop entering any exhibits.

My mother sometimes picked a piece of fruit without anyone's daring to repoach her. If Daphne, Ralph or I wanted an apple or pear, we would go in search of Mr Hill and beg him to unlock the apple or pear houses for us, so that we could select from the slatted, damp-free, airy shelves some fruit gathered from the enormous variety that grew on our standards, bushes, pergolas or espaliers.

Most of the fruit was in the kitchen garden across a country lane, in cool glass houses and in half a dozen hot houses. The latter were heated by four-inch pipes which led from two furnaces and ran along the ground under the windows. Two or three large trucks of anthracite were run to Wimborne Station every year, then hauled to Kingston Lacy by the farm people. The coal, some knobs weighing half-a-hundred weight, was stacked by the stoves. The gardeners would keep the fires going all day, banking them up at ten o'clock at night to last until half past six the next morning, when they would cycle up the gravel road from the village to stoke them again.

Each hot house contained a large tank filled with cool water, whose floating balls for the stopcocks we would press down for fun as we passed. The hot houses produced fragile, exotic orchids, leafy bougainvilia and soft blue, phlox-like plumbago, yellow guavas and melons trained to grow upright on the walls. There were all kinds of berries in mouthwatering profusion, even huge, sweet strawberries in February, as well as both red and white raspberries, red and green gooseberries and purple loganberries.

In the cool houses, a few months after the cascades of filmy pink blossom which filled the huge windows in spring had made a decaying carpet on the ground, there followed all the stone fruit you could imagine: nectarines, apricots, black and white cherries. Fifteen hundred peaches were produced in a season, each ripe peach being kept for only four days.

Tempting red and yellow miniature 'bananas' growing on a spiky leafed bush behind the house opposite the stables were poisonous, but who needed bananas when they could eat the green figs which grew in an unheated glasshouse on the lawn, twice the size of figs you see in shops today.

'You mustn't do too much cutting out with figs,' said the

gardeners, 'or you will spoil the fruit.'

A short, rather square man with an unusually long stride, Mr Hill, the head gardener, was feared and hated by all the under gardeners, whom he would fiercely threaten with his gun if they should make a mistake and break off a shoot unintentionally. However, he was very fond of us children and would let us tease him and hang onto his gardener's short, stubby fingers as we walked along. Like a father, he would patiently watch us stand on our heads in the gym field – a strange sight, no doubt, in our ordinary 'undies'. He also advised Daphne and me in the cultivation of our own plots. These were next to the kitchen garden in the flower garden, divided by a high, old yew hedge from the part where the flowers for cutting were grown, including a quarter of an acre of bulbs – daffodils, narcissi, jonquils and tulips. Ralph was never at home long enough, once his school days had started, to keep up with gardening, but Daphne and I industriously dug and planted and hoed, delighted to see our flowers obediently springing up. I grew violas, of course, and pansies, blue scabious, hyacinths and a variety of vivid annuals.

One day, on our way back to the house with Jim, the wire haired terrier, after working our little plots of garden, we heard strange male yells and ran back to where the sound came from. One of the gardeners, a ruddy complexioned, brown-haired man of about thirty, always rather aloof, who had been digging where the lettuces grew, was lying on his back in his black trousers and jacket, his cloth cap beside him on the soil, shouting unintelligibly, and writhing from side to side. We ran back to the potting shed where Snell, my favourite gardener, was busy and begged him to go to the afflicted man.

'He's all right, Miss.' he muttered and went on potting.

Country attitudes to epilepsy were obviously very matter of fact, though it was probably quite dangerous to leave the victim to struggle back to normality on his own.

In addition to the glasshouses of flowers, where a yellow form of mimosa shone like sunlight, there were cool frames where immense *Marie Louise* Parma violets grew to make a posy for my mother's corsage, enlivening her eternal stiff black taffeta blouse for church on Sunday, before being put into a vase on the desk in the library. My mother had had great lavender hedges planted in the kitchen garden round areas of grass and parterres. She also had built two summer houses, at both entrances to the garden, where she could sit on warm days in her large black hat and gaze at the flowers.

Mr Hill was always bad tempered on Saturdays, when he was irritated at having to part with some of his precious flowers for church decoration. He regarded flowers and fruit as primarily for my mother's delectation in the house, though he did not begrudge the large basket of fruit which was regularly sent to our anaemic and unhealthy-looking family doctor.

The only occasion on which my mother really hurt Mr Hill was during the incident of the chrysanthemum cuttings. Every gardener, even on an estate as vast as Kingston Lacy, where there was such a huge variety of magnificent blooms, has one flower or shrub or vegetable which he cherishes above all others. With Mr Hill it was chrysanthemums. He and his gardeners spent hours and hours on them until my mother finally became impatient and put a stop to it.

'A thousand pots of chrysanthemums are far too many. You must cut them down to two hundred,' she demanded.

If we were lucky to be surrounded by so many growing things, we were perhaps even more fortunate, as children, to have so many animals close to us. The only captive wild creatures were the rabbits which the cook-housekeeper kept and the Iberian or Asiatic brown owl that my father had caught as a young bird on his travels abroad. It lived in the maze or fernery in a house which had two compartments, one open and one curtained. Charlie Hart used to look after it, throwing it rats and mice he had caught. It lived for a long time, coming out from behind its curtain and looking at us if we made a noise, giving a flap or two, then going back in disgust if we had not brought it a mouse. It was obligatory for all visitors to come and admire our strange bird.

Country children were not allowed to be sentimental about animals, even if we might be tempted to think of them in a cosy, nursery way. For instance, when we persuaded 'Boysie' (Ralph) to get his hoops and join us down the Wimborne Drive, which was wide enough for three, he would recite an absurd little jingle:

All the little rabbits,
So engaging in their habits,
They all have a hole but me, but me.

Yet we knew that a rabbit's burrow was no defence from Boast, the keeper. We could not avoid seeing him going out with his gun, terrier and ferrets.

Despite Boast's hardness towards wild creatures, he looked rather like an amiable beaver himself, with head thrust forward, large nose and reddish brown skin. His insensitivity to the feelings of animals extended to his own unfortunate black retriever who never seemed to be off the lead. Poor dog! He would always come out of his kennel and hopefully wag his tail when he saw us. Yet it would not have been thought right for us to take him out or ask that he should be let off his chain more often.

The keeper, who was well-disposed enough to us, failed to understand our feelings for wild birds. Finding blackbird and thrushes' nests in the box bushes in the woods at the sides of the Ladies' Walk, we would pop little pieces of home-made white bread soaked in milk into the gaping beaks of the nestlings. I wonder what the mother bird thought when she returned, exhausted with looking for worms, and found them not hungry!

If the eggs had not already hatched, we would carefully take out just one for our collection which was housed in a small nest of drawers, each egg neatly labelled with type and the date when found, on minute pieces of stamp paper. When the well-meaning keeper heard about our collection, he brought us four skylarks' eggs, greyish-white, speckled with brown, which distressed us very much. It is rare to find a lark's nest, for they are always built of dried grass in a hollow on the ground and carefully hidden. Even if you watch a lark land and hurry to the spot, you will not find the nest. The bird alights some distance away and runs to it through the grass. The keeper must have completely emptied the nest he had found. All the eggs were cracked, because he had put them into his pocket. We did not tell him, but they were no good for our collection of carefully blown, perfect specimens.

It was taken for granted that every squire had his own shoot. At Kingston Lacy, pheasants' eggs were put under hens in coops at the gamekeeper's cottage to be hatched. In my father's time, shooting parties were frequent. Our neighbours driving over from their own estates, their carriages being put up for the whole day or for the night and their horses fed and rested before the return journey. In addition, there were sometimes fifty people staying in the house, every guest bringing a maid or valet to swell the already large household and gossip about his or her employer.

After my father's death, when Ralph was still a minor, the shooting was leased to a tenant, Mr Spiller, who though he was a retired sugar planter looked as if he came from Lapland, with his long Santa Claus white beard. In fact, he did spend the winter fishing in Norway each year. He was occasionally spotted by Daphne and me as we trotted on our horses with Mr Crook, the coachman, on the grass beside the Blandford Drive, *en route* for Badbury Rings or the rabbit-riddled Crichel Downs. Except for his beard and his grey-green Norfolk tweed hat, jacket, knickerbokers and woollen stockings to protect him from nettles, he looked like a Stonehenge monolith, very erect, gun on shoulder pointing down in the correct manner, with a keeper and two dogs who barked at us on our own ground.

'There's Mr Spiller,' we would say to each other and to Mr Crook, who took off his bowler hat. Mr Spiller would also raise his hat as we went by. Daphne and I would turn to smile shyly in his direction, too young to have yet learnt to bow gracefully from our saddles. We kept at a distance since dogs and horses do not always agree and my pony, 'Silvertail,' who indulged in capers at the least flutter of a bird in the hedge, was far too ladylike to permit of a strange dog sniffing at her heels.

Mr Spiller lived in Pamphill Manor, a red brick Georgian house supposedly haunted by a lady in grey. It was said that someone put a rope across the stairs one night and she walked right through it. Mr Spiller, down-to-earth sportsman that he was, was not in the least troubled by her. He was more inclined to smoke his pipe over his *Morning Post* than to concern himself with the supernatural and never appeared in our church on Sundays. When shooting in the

Park, in late summer and autumn, he always remembered to send us a polite warning not to ride across his guns in case we were shot.

When we were children and entered the house by the back door we used to peer fearfully into the larder outside the kitchen where the gamekeeper hung up the game he had shot for the table: pheasants, wild duck, teal, hares, rabbits and pigeons. My father, who was fond of rabbit pie, was quoted as saying, 'Young rabbits, hard-boiled eggs and good pastry are a feast for the gods.'

Being a sportsman, he did not despise what he had shot, though the servants, much more fastidious, classed rabbits and pigeon as vermin and would not eat them.

The Red Devons and the sheep alternately provided sirloin and saddle of lamb for our Sunday lunch and the Home Farm supplied us with pork and poultry. Nevertheless, we felt great affection for the animals. A farm in those days was a place of great charm, not just a factory for food production. There were pigs to feed, cows to milk, hens whose eggs we could feel for in the hollows of tree trunks, and beautiful old shire horses to fondle.

Our bailiff, Mr Haytor, would never have survived in the world of modern commercial farming. He was good-natured and honest and, despite his name, perfectly benevolent. His wife, who always seemed miraculously to have a glass of warm fresh milk ready for us, was equally friendly. She was rosy-cheeked and enormously fat, with two solitary teeth which showed when she smiled.

The Haytors put up with us children with stoical heroism, considering that our Pekinese used to so enjoy harrassing the elderly milking cows and our own clumsy tumbling about was hard on the tender nerves of the broody hens. I once fell into the pig manure in my Sunday frock and had to be rescued and cleaned up before reappearing at the house. The Haytors were unvaryingly welcoming, though they must have anticipated our frequent visits with dread.

Our own domestic pets were not the most fortunate of animals. In addition to the early demise of my bob-tailed sheepdog, probably of distemper, Ralph's fox terrier puppy swallowed a bee and died instantly. Daphne's wire-haired terrier, Jim, was silently and mysteriously replaced by the Pekinese.

However, horses were the animals which played the largest part in my life at Kingston Lacy. I had graduated from a donkey to a tame Shetland pony of which I have only the haziest memory. We had four other Shetlands later: 'George', 'Mary', 'M'Lord' and 'M'Lady,' given to us by Lord and Lady Bristol who had bred them but had not broken them in. No one ever succeeded in training any of them except for the smallest, 'M'Lady,' who did pull a cart and allowed Ralph to ride her.

Beloved by me above all the animals on the estate was my own beautiful mare, 'Silvertail,' bred by my father from a New Forest pony and an Arab. Her mouth was as hard as steel so that she was not ideal for a child to learn on. She was very lovable but had a will of iron so that often, when I had a collected canter in mind, I was forced to enjoy a mad gallop instead. I frequently fell off her on the downs, letting her trip in a shallow rift in the turf. Secretly ashamed of the mishap, I would breezily announce at lunch: 'I fell off again today.'

My mother would take the news very lightly, probably from frequent repetition and, after all, it was not Ralph who had fallen off. Like the sheepdog, 'Silvertail' vanished from my life without explanation, though I was by then in my teens. The conspiracy of silence continued.

Normally our horses would be prepared ready for us to ride and brought to the mounting block. When my mother was away, however, formality ceased and we children could join in the working life of the stable. We learned to groom the horses, though we did not quite perfect the hiss with which Mr Crook the coachman did it.

Outside in the centre of the stable yard was a disused pump with a tiled roof. Built round the yard were the horse boxes, harness room and grooms' quarters. The stables were painted dark, reddish-brown and were roomy but warm, smelling richly of horses and leather. Above was a loft with rooms in which the menservants slept.

When Royalty or other special visitors came they were always given sugar to feed the horses, so Mr Crook would decorate the stables and horse boxes with plaited straw and ribbon rosettes. Each of the six horse boxes had bars in front in a passageway, with a manger at the other end against the wall. Crook was very proud of two doors covered with horse shoes and the names and dates of my father's winning race horses, especially the most famous of all, 'Tilly Whim,' who had won the Derby.

It must have been sad for Crook when my father died, since it was he who had found his future coachman wandering vaguely, aged about sixteen, on the race course at Newmarket, not even knowing what his own name was. My father had christened him 'Crook' and brought him back to Kingston Lacy where he had worked for fifty-two years. He taught us all to ride, to hunt and how to perilously drive the ponycart through the narrow twisting streets of Wimborne to fetch the groceries, often leaning over to snatch the reins when we were about to catch the wheel of a neighbouring cart.

Crook was very proud of his spick and span coach house full of carriages, carts, chaises, landaus, wagonettes and hansom cab. He always drove sitting outside each vehicle in the open air, without any protection from the elements except his greatcoat and a bowler hat, or a top hat if he was driving my mother. It was surprising, considering his love of horses, that he got on quite amicably with the chauffeur, Mr Brain, when my mother bought a roomy, dark blue Wolseley car in 1908. Brain was much more modern and would reply to my mother's orders with a, 'Yes, Madam. Very good, Madam,' in contrast with the coachman's traditional and respectful. 'Yes M'.'

With the arrival of the car, we immediately lost interest in driving the ponycart. Even the wagonette was no longer used except for picnics, taking hot food out to a shooting party, or collecting luggage from the station so that it would not scratch the shining car.

When old Mr Crook was dying, Daphne, who was always the kind, good member of the family, went to his bedroom in the stables to see him. I was too embarrassed to go because I had never seen a man in bed. He begged to see the little squire, but Ralph, indulged as usual, was not made to visit him.

Right up to the end, Mr Crook had spent all his money on racing. His widow was not given a pension. None of the servants at Kingston Lacy ever were. The only time any regular charitable payment was made was during the 1914-18 war, when all the gardeners who had joined the Dorset Yeomanry were paid half-wages, while their places were kept open for them. Sadly, I cannot remember seeing any of them when the war was over.

After her husband's death, Mrs Crook was told she could work in the house if she liked. She felt it demeaning however and soon left. It was probably a mercy for Mr. Crook that he died before we caught the roller-skating craze in Paris, for my mother cleared all his precious carriages out of the coach house and turned its concrete floor into a rather uneven rink.

5
A Wintry Chapter

Except for Royal visits, when we were very much part of the event, we, as small children, had little to do with our mother's guests. We might be put on show for a few minutes, then whisked away again before the visitors could become bored with us. Most of the time we led our private, carefree lives, paying little attention to Mama's entourage of ambassadors, artists or society beauties. Any unwary visitor who did find his way upstairs to the school room would be very successfully discouraged by having our missionary box, with its picture of a ragged street urchin, like a Murillo boy, rattled imperiously at him until he dropped in a shilling.

Only Canon Sowter braved the missionary box with any regularity. Tall, tanned, upright and distinguished, with twinkling grey eyes and a charming smile, wearing a glossy top hat and carrying a folded umbrella, his first words to' my mother when he had met her in charge of a stall at a Wimborne charity bazaar with Daphne and me had been, 'Are the little girls for sale?'

Having no children of his own, which was a great sorrow to him, he loved us all. Though he was a Canon of Salisbury Cathedral, he often lunched with us at Kingston Lacy. We were delighted to see him, except for the fact that if Miss Tidmarsh knew he was coming she would always make us learn the Collect of the day by heart so we could recite it to him.

Canon Sowter gave us a *Stories from the Gospels* book, Mrs Ewing's *Flat Iron for a Farthing* and all her other books, leather bound, in a cardboard case. One day, his wife, probably beginning to sense his deep, though hermetically concealed, love for Mama, came to us in tears. They had received a bill for £40 from a bookshop. I must confess that we children enjoyed the books less than the cheap papers, *The Scout* (enthralling!) and *The Garden*, that we had every week. We could never take the Canon's poor, white-faced wife seriously, because of her extraordinarily large hats, the *pince-nez* perched on her hooked nose and the rasping voice in which she always called her husband, 'Francis dear'. Not even her distraught visit halted the Canon's reckless extravagance. He bought all the volumes of a children's encyclopaedia for us as they came out and had them beautifully bound.

We children never thought about having to earn our livings in later life. There was no reason to doubt that we would always have friendly, helpful people taking care of our every need. I shed the odd, sentimental tear at the thought of marrying one day and leaving Mummy, but Winnie, a nurserymaid, reassured me that it was, 'Too soon to think about that yet, Cis, m'dear.'

In those days, because mourning continued for years, there were no entertainments at Kingston Lacy. We did not feel the lack of them. The three of us created our own. We would put on shows for the whole staff, indoor and out, in the housekeeper's still-room. Such well-trained servants could be relied upon to smile good naturedly as we forgot our lines, giggled or turned our backs.

Not so our mother! Our ineptitude as performers was as annoying to her as our enthusiasm for special effects. Once we put black plaster on Ralph's front teeth and turned him into such a realistically toothless woodcutter that Mama thought his precious second teeth were gone for ever.

'I do not want you to act any more plays,' she said, when it was over. 'It is much too painful.'

Amateur theatricals had to wait until our enjoyable visits to Lord and Lady Digby's family at Minterne, their rambling, early eighteenth-century house which had formerly belonged to the Churchills. It was high in the hills at Minterne Magna, the Great Hintock of Thomas Hardy's novels, near Cerne Abbas.

The Digby's were a large and hospitable family who loved having a house full of children. Lady Digby (Beryl to my mother) was tall and elegant. Her husband was something of a naturalist and once showed us under a microscope, tiny, stirring mites he had just discovered in the cheese. The childen's governess, Mademoiselle Pasteur, and trim Miss Tidmarsh, used to go out for walks together when we stayed at Minterne or when the Digby's returned our visits.

Fair, blue-eyed Geraldine, the second Digby daughter and always referred to as 'G', was Daphne's friend and the first of all of us to marry, to an officer in the Grenadier Guards. Lettice, my friend, tall, with straight long hair and a fresh complexion, who behaved very correctly, was about five years older than me and therefore seemed very interesting. Little, sandy-haired Venetia, the third daughter, was the odd one out. Both she and her younger rosy-cheeked brother, Bob, followed me about adoringly, in the most boring fashion. Our laundrymaids decided that I would marry the eldest son, Kenelm, who was very shy and polite and not at all exciting as far as I was concerned. The laundrymaids did their best to stir up some enthusiasm in me for him by walking into Wimborne to buy me a Valentine card which they could pretend he had sent me.

At Minterne we were always impressed by the writing

paper – which though it was in our bedrooms we were banned from using – because it had Lord Digby's baronial coronet on it. We also learned to dress formally. We once shocked our Nanny by asking, in loud astonished voices, what sashes were, when she took them out for us to put on our dresses.

There were no children's parties at Kingston Lacy, which made those of the Portmans, the Normantons, the Alingtons and the Shaftesburys seem all the more magnificent. A vast number of carriages would converge on their large houses, many grown-ups accompanying the children. Mothers waited impatiently in vast cloakrooms, while Nannies took off wraps, smoothed dresses crushed from the long drives behind the carriage horses, and brushed hair.

At the Alington's Christmas party at Crichel House near Wimborne the huge Christmas tree which rose to the lofty ceiling seemed as high as the tree in Trafalgar Square and was completely covered with presents wrapped in brown or tissue paper tied with brightly ribboned bows. We played treasure hunts for specially hidden chocolates, ate a disgracefully large tea (though our nurse would not let us eat any of the great iced and cream cake handed round by the butler and a footman) then staggered onto the polished floor to dance. Daphne and I, shy and tongue-tied, would envy the assurance of the other child guests; high-spirited Lois Sturt, Lady Alington's daughter, and fair, quiet Cyriel Bulkely, both of whom resembled little angels. A suave gentleman of five or six, in an Eton suit, asked me to dance and behaved with such gallantry that I was at a loss as how to respond.

On the way home, wrapped to the cheeks in heavy, white shawls, we would fall asleep while the horses, refreshed after their rest and feed, would step out fast for their warm stable at Kingston Lacy.

Children's parties were tame compared with our more adventurous games at Kingston Lacy, wild paper chases through the woods and fields, restricted only by our mother's stern proviso, 'You must not drop paper in the grounds.'

When other childen were staying with us, 'Sardines' and 'hide and seek' could go on interminably in the candlelit gloom. You could find yourself hysterically huddled in a whispering, giggling heap of children in a dark, old cupboard in a bedroom or, suddenly, totally alone, feeling very foolish, knowing that every single child but you had found the companionable hiding place. Nobody ever failed to be found in the end or was discovered, years later, in skeletal form, like young Lovel's bride in *The Mistletoe Bough*, but why did my mother mysteriously refer to our ancient oak chest as 'the one in which Barbara Hyde died.'? I have never found out.

I loved winter at Kingston Lacy. With the park under frost, the trees formed an intricate tracery of bare, white branches. When we grazed our knees on the frozen earth we knew that the foxes would be safe, for there was never any hunting when the ground was hard. Deeper into winter, the heavy snows would seal us in, till the gardeners cleared a track from the house to the Wimborne Lodge, just wide enough for the sturdy wagonette. The cedar trees suffered most of all, losing their tops in the high winds, but the tall copper beech near the lodge gates proudly withstood all storms.

If the winter was severe we had snow-lions in the garden, instead of snowmen, for the bronze lions from Herculanium in front of the terrace were never protected by covers – unlike the pink marble lionesses at the foot of the terrace steps which disappeared under mundane shelters, like hen coops, and did not re-emerge till Spring.

One winter, when the ice was thick, Alfred Lodder, the son of the agent to the estate, took Daphne and me to Pamphill Pond to skate. Eli Ricketts from the Vine Inn had swept the snow from the ice and the pond was full of skating villagers who respectfully moved to one side when they saw us coming. An obliging cottager offered two kitchen chairs. Though we did not perform any figures of eight or dainty arabesques, and though pushing a wooden chair in front of one is not the most elegant way to skate, we thought we put on quite a good show for beginners. Alfred Lodder picked us up when we fell down and everyone was much too polite to laugh.

Kingston Lacy could be very cold in winter. The upstairs fireplaces were too small to make much difference to the overall temperature so, when the gong thundered through the house for tea, we hurtled down four flights of stairs, followed by the governess, to the warm, panelled dining room, for scones and fresh bread with strawberry or peach jam from our own fruit. Here was the only radiator in the house, as well as a huge log fire.

The first sign that Christmas was coming was the appearance of old Mrs Lush with her boxes of Christmas cards, which first the servants chose from, then we children rummaged through, picking out all those with fat, red-breasted robins on them, or pink-faced little girls in the snow, wearing fur edged hats and coats and fluffy muffs. Ralph liked pictures of horses pulling a stage coach or of London streets under snow, lit by glowing lamps.

Next the gardeners would arrive with armfuls of holly and mistletoe. We were not allowed to decorate the main part of the house because of the risk of fire or of spoiling the paintings, but we decorated every corner of the school-room and nursery.

Then came the hard work. Daphne and I would begin our mass production of presents for our mother's many friends. Miss Tidmarsh taught us to make little old women pen wipers out of chickens' wishbones, dressed in red and black flounces of cloth with sealing wax eyes. We made lavender bags from the lavender we had collected and dried to give to all the men who came to stay to put in their linen.

Finally, we all went down to the kitchen to stir Jinky's enormous plum pudding mixture, one after another, each making a secret wish.

We all hung up our stockings on Christmas Eve, always wide awake and always simulating deep sleep when our mother came in later to fill them. She invariably put an orange in the toe, crackers and biscuits above and, on top, a present. That was where I had found my picture of the little girl reading, that hung opposite my bed.

When we awoke on Christmas Day, the *jardinières* in the drawing room and saloon were overflowing with brilliant hot house plants, the gardeners having crept in at seven thirty, as they did twice a week, to look after the house plants, changing into slippers and creeping round the house so as not to disturb anybody.

We went to church on Christmas morning, then, for the rest of the day, were allowed to do what we liked. We walked to the gardens and the farm with Mama. One year, in an improvised darkroom (which had once been the lady's maids room and was now the playroom) we spent the afternoon developing pictures we had taken of Mama's guests, printing the photographs by the light of the great schoolroom windows. When the daylight failed, we pored over our favourite books by lamplight.

When I was twelve, I climbed up to light the Christmas tree candles, then, having drunk a little too much champagne, slid woozily all the way down to the bottom of the tall stepladder. Nobody took much notice.

Our mother tried her best to make Christmas a festive season. As we grew older, she failed, despite all the traditional food and drink, because Daphne and I had no friends of our own there, and felt their lack. Ralph's gauche Etonian friends were allowed to stay with us but were too young to be intriguing or gallant. I still feel sad when I remember that one Christmas in my early twenties I stayed away from Kingston Lacy altogether, attracted elsewhere by brighter company.

The servants did not have a party, though they did have a Christmas dinner with beef instead of turkey. At nine o'clock, they lined up along one side of the dining room in hierarchical order to receive their excruciatingly dull presents. These were a length of cloth for each woman, either black for Sunday or cheerful flowered cotton for everyday, to be made up at their own expense, and a box of chocolates. The men were each given ten shillings and a box or a bottle of port. Daphne and I who made the presentations, were embarrassed at giving such uninteresting gifts, avoiding the eyes of the servants who stood there trying to look suitably grateful.

Mother was more imaginative where our presents were concerned. She gave us books at Easter, New Year and Christmas, often beautifully bound. There were always other gifts too. I remember a framed oil picture of a girl's head and a travelling alarm clock in purple leather being given to me when I was thirteen. Her presents sometimes paled a little beside those of Mrs Jenks, or Jinky, the cook, which were magnificent and showed her fondness for us: silver hair brushes, silver photograph frames or cut glass bottles of perfume.

We children would give our mother perfectly superfluous 'marquetry' gifts, since she already possessed everything she could possibly want. We engraved or burnt patterns on wooden articles, matchboxes or the handles of paper knives. We also swopped presents amongst ourselves. Ralph once gave me a round, grey leather man's collar box with strings that pulled it together, in which I kept cotton reels. Another time he presented me with a silver stamp box with *'Stamps'* engraved on the lid, which my mother must have bought for him since, even then, silver was expensive.

The last event of Christmas Day to look forward to would be family dinner, when roast turkey, carved by Mr Cooper at the buffet beside the serving lift, partly hidden by a fifteenth-century tapestry on the wall, would be accompanied by chestnut and sausage stuffing, sprouts and roast potatoes. After this would arrive Jinky's plum pudding, borne aloft, flaming with brandy, by Mr Cooper.

Just as we were raising our knives and forks ready to begin the meal, word would be brought that the carol singers had arrived. Grudgingly we would leave our hot turkey, cross over the passage through the cool Alabaster Room where the fruit was kept, into the lighted Spanish Room, where we stood at the window and tried to look pleased while the village choir sang their hearts out on the gravel drive in front of the porch. Mr Cooper would welcome them into the kitchen for hot drinks, mince pies and money, while we rushed back to our interrupted, luke-warm Christmas meal. When the dishes were all cleared away we would open our presents which would be laid out on the dining room table.

Another member of the Bankes family was always thought

of kindly at Christmas. Mama ignored all our other cousins but considered that Jerome Bankes, next in line after Ralph to inherit, was of some importance. Each year she sent him a huge hamper of every type of Christmas fare imaginable, even a turkey. He, for his part, would give us delicious hand-made chocolates. Then, one day, a remark made by Jerome was passed on to my mother;

'I shall probably have Kingston Lacy one day. Ralph is a very sickly boy and not likely to live.'

Although his Christmas hampers stopped abruptly. Jerome lived to a great old age, writing to Childe's Bank annually for his pension, with the message: 'I regret to say I am still alive.'

Ralph outlived him by many years.

6

Life below stairs

Our mother, fortunately for us, for it gave us whole, blissful weeks of freedom from her critical surveillance, was a
hypochondriac. No sooner had Mr Crook driven her out
through the iron gates on the first leg of her journey to
Marienbad in Germany for a 'cure' (which consisted of
drinking water which tasted like rotten eggs and receiving
massage) than all strict protocol at Kingston Lacy was relaxed. We children rushed down the back stairs to the
flagstoned kitchen to celebrate her departure with the servants.

The kitchen was a light, cheerful room overlooking the
shrubbery. Right down the centre was a large, white deal
table, on which most of the food was prepared. In one
corner stood a high tripod with metal shelves where bur-
nished copper saucepans ranged in height shone like stars.
One end was filled by a big dresser, on which stood Brown-
Bessie teapots in every size, and china breakfast and tea
services.

This was the empire of tiny, bustling, smiling Mrs Jenks,
always dressed in a white ribbed cotton or linen dress and
white apron with a white 'rubber' or cloth pinned over her
bosom and tied behind for cooking. She wore a horsehair
pad on her head, unsuccessfully disguised by her own hair
which she combed over it. She regulated everything downstairs in the most capable fashion, giving her kitchen maids
an excellent training. She was delighted to see us, busily
involving us in whatever activity was going on. She taught

us how to make pastry.

'Handle it as little as possible, Miss Cissie', she would say, 'Keep it cool. Don't add too much water, Miss Daphne. Roll it very lightly.'

This was much too subtle for us. Our intractable mixture would sometimes be so sticky that, when we took it out of the huge oven, or 'Kitchener', fed by coal and logs, that ran halfway along the west wall, it would be depressingly hard or solid. On other occasions we would have stretched it so much that it would spring back like elastic in the cooking, leaving steak and kidney, apples or gooseberries exposed in an unseemly way all round the edges. We never did succeed in turning out light, crumbly pie crusts like Jinky's. Dear Jinky never minded the floury mess we made in the kitchen any more than she objected to our creeping down-stairs in the middle of the night after some energetic dance in London, in our débutante years, to raid her newly stocked larder. We would wash our hands in the kitchen sink using long bars of primrose yellow soap or a tablet of 'Monkey' brand, the wrapper of which had a monkey's face on it.

Before coming to Kingston Lacy, Jinky had catered for high society on board Solly Joel's yacht, the *Eileen*, on its frequent, glittering cruises along the Riviera. Solly Joel was a well-known Jewish coal, copper, gold and diamond mil-lionaire, whose interests also included the theatre, cricket and horseracing; his horse, 'Bachelor's Button', having begun a whole series of wins for him when it had beaten the celebrated 'Pretty Polly' in the Ascot Gold Cup in 1906. He was renowned for his lavish hospitality, obviously largely owing to the culinary skills of Jinky. There was absolutely nothing she could not cook, from game to goose-berry fool.

We loved to follow her into the bakery beyond the kitchen and watch her gently press a ball of dough down in the middle with her fist before shaping it into a loaf, or carefully grate flakes of brown nutmeg onto a creamy rice pudding mixture meant for us. Twice a week, on Tuesday and Friday, Edward Dukes, a deferential young gardener's boy, destined eventually to become head gardener, would bring fresh fruit and vegetables to the kitchen door. Basketfuls of old fashioned, black winter spinach were finely puréed through wire sieves, tender young runner beans sliced paper thin and potatoes made to look like rice, all served up, when our mother was in residence, in magnificently polished silver dishes with silver compartments and silver lids.

Fortunately, in order to withstand the chill of the great, unheated, stoneflagged Servants' Hall and of their comfortless attics, the servants would have been ever ready to eat up all the left overs. There was a kitchenmaid in a blue cotton dress and white apron, a scullery maid who wore a pink dress under the white apron, in addition to the housemaids and the nurserymaid who took her meals in the nursery with us. As well as the butler, there was always an extra footman to help Ernest Masters, the regular footman, when there were parties of forty or fifty guests upstairs. There were also several men who worked out of doors.

The servants had their official dinner time before ours, sitting at a long table in the Servants' Hall in hierarchical order, butler at one end, each man (though not each maid) with his half pint bottle of beer beside his plate. Noisily trooping upstairs the back way, we children would peep through the door and grin at our own special favourites, as they sat in complete and decorous silence over their first course, unable to smile back. Mr Cooper, the butler, would preside, carving their joints of meat (cheaper cuts than ours) which were accompanied by mounds of potatoes, before retiring to join Mrs Jenks in the housekeeper's still-room to eat his 'Spotted Dick' or Roly-Poly pudding with home-made raspberry jam.

The servants might well have been ravenous after a day of toil which both they and we took for granted. There was endless polishing of floors, furniture and silver, washing of mountains of linen in the laundry and carrying of meals between kitchen and dining room or up the four flights of steps to the nursery. The men had to bring in coal and logs to stoke the many fires and feed the two great boilers, one by the kitchen, the other by the butler's pantry near the marble staircase, which warmed the four inch hot water pipes for heating and domestic use.

No doubt there was much more work to be done in addition, of which we three children remained blissfully unaware.

Though their bedrooms were three bedded, unheated comfortless attics, the maids did have a warm room where they could sit together chatting at a round mahogany 'loo' table (so-called after the card game 'loo' or 'lanterloo' for which it was designed) sewing the house linen. Daphne and I would peer through the door but, even when Mama was away, the maids never invited us into this private domain. They were not given the luxury of a bathroom when a very simple one was installed for us, but continued to bath in a tub as we had done in the nursery, though without the comfort of a fire.

Not being so carefully supervised when Mama was away, it was much easier to slip away past the maids' rooms onto the roof which had a parapet all round and was quite safe, though strictly forbidden. We could see for miles, right over the Park almost to Badbury Rings. It was also a convenient time to explore the lumber-room.

Once, ferreting among the dusty trunks and cases, Daphne and I came upon a long, coffin-like tin box. Breathlessly, we raised the lid and discovered, so we thought, the mouldering remains of our dead father's bones, disintegrating among the folds of his scarlet sheriff's robes. Many years went by before we dared to reveal our ghoulish secret, only to be informed that the sinister, decaying bones were dried apples put into the robes to deter the moths.

The house was isolated so there were never any parties below stairs. The servants were only too ready to go to bed at nine o'clock, their day having begun at half past five in the morning. It was, nevertheless, regarded as a great privilege and often a cherished family tradition to work at Kingston Lacy and it was very rarely that anyone left. Edward Dukes rejected an opportunity to be articled to a lawyer in Wimborne, preferring to follow in his father's footsteps and train in our gardens, which offered tremendous scope, and which many regarded as being second in importance only to Kew. Even the humblest and most hardworked kitchen maids were attached to our mother and considered themselves fortunate to be working for her for £12 a year.

Another reason why servants stayed employed so long was that they could rarely afford to marry and often were courting for years. One marriage did take place while we were children: Fred Pope, a footman, sometimes referred to as 'the odd man', whose tasks varied from polishing the family's shoes to bringing up salt water from Studland Bay for Ralph's bath when we were on holiday, married a kitchen maid, Bessie Paine.

Fred was a clumsy, golden hearted giant. Bessie was fairhaired and blue-eyed, dainty and neat. With a child's artless, open-eyed curiosity, I used to question Bessie about her deeply ribbed fingernails:

'Bessie, why are your nails like that?'

'I'm sure I don't know, Miss,' Bessie would say and hurry about her work. No one ever thought in terms of vitamins, protein or calories. Fred and Bessie had to leave us when they married, for there were no married quarters at Kingston Lacy.

All the washing of the family's and servants' linen was done, all day and everyday, by two Irish laundrymaids. The sheets, washed without chemicals and carried in huge, heavy baskets to be hung out of sight behind the stables, would emerge beautifully soft and fresh. There were two laundry rooms in a low building along one side of the courtyard with a semi-covered passage from the back door. We could look down into them from the backstairs landing or visit them, especially if our mother was away. In one room, kind Julia, who was pitifully thin, and good-natured Ellen, who was enormously fat, washed all the linen in a vast boiler. In the other room they did the ironing, heating the flat irons on a stove and holding them up to their cheeks to see if they were hot.

Julia and Ellen were sisters, devout Catholics who walked the five miles to the nearest Catholic church every Sunday. Father O'Flynn, the parish priest, who looked like Friar Tuck, would often come on a pastoral visit and chat to them through the open laundry windows as they worked, leaning with his arms on the window sill. Daphne and I would walk past, staring at his black back and at our friends' radiant faces as they hung on his words.

Such strange happiness was perhaps irritating and somewhat disturbing to the other servants. They jealously made up a rhyme supposed to be a lament by Ellen:

'Father O'Flynn, agin and agin,
I thought you loved me dearly,
But sorrow! I find
Ye've changed your mind
'Tis darling *Julia* O'Leary.'

This spiteful teasing must eventually have driven the two sisters away. Very early one morning the nurserymaid called me to say that they had come down from their bedroom, to the floor where the nursery and schoolroom were to say goodbye. Years later, after I myself had become a Catholic, I mentioned in confession one of my greatest sorrows. Callous little girl that I was, or shy at the thought of an emotional leave-taking, I had asked the nurserymaid to tell the two departing laundrymaids that I was still asleep.

Past the laundry in the courtyard where Mr Shears sawed the logs from the estate was 'Galpin's lair', the electric room where huge vats of acid stood which the electrician, Mr Galphin, warned us never to touch. How we longed, but did not dare, to drop a handkerchief into a vat and see it magically eaten away!

When Mama was abroad, in addition to having free run of the house, we were able to stay up much later than usual. On winter evenings, Mr Cooper, the butler, and Ralph would play billiards quite expertly, neither of them ever cutting the cloth, or Daphne, Mr Cooper, Mr Crook and I would sit up in the library playing whist.

If it was summer, we played cricket on the side of the lawn nearest the Park, where Jinky kept her hens and chickens, so as not to spoil the smooth surface of the main lawn. We easily made up an eleven with the staff from the kitchen, the pantry, the garage and the coachhouse, playing until the light faded and moths flew against our faces.

Mr Crook with his short, horseman's legs was always run out, never reaching the wicket in time, or else he would be bowled out first ball, leg before wicket. In contrast, Mr Cooper, the butler, would score more runs than anyone else and was a demon bowler, taking a short run, the tip of his tongue laid along his lower lip, and throwing the ball under-arm with amazing speed.

'Come on, Cis!' Ralph would shout as he sped towards my wicket.

'Just do it!' we, youngest and fleetest of the cricket eleven, muttered breathlessly as we passed each other, bat in hand.

Even Mr Hervey, the dignified but absent-minded trustee of Kingston Lacy during Ralph's minority, would catch the holiday spirit and play croquet with us in his green tweed waistcoat and trousers. If possible, without quite under-standing who he was, we would casually mention Keir Hardie, founder of the Labour party, Keir Hardie's name being sufficient to drive Hervey into such a rage that his sporting ability was impaired.

Mr Cooper, who perfected the training of the other ser-vants, was, himself, a treasure beyond words. My mother could never have entertained as she did without him. Al-ways dressed in black, he was the perfect butler in every word and gesture, never for one moment stepping out of place, however much we teased him. His facial expression never altered to express annoyance or surprise though his whole body respectfully conveyed shocked disapproval at the familiarity of Canon Sowter, who insisted on shaking hands with him at the front door.

As a very young boy, Cooper had been page to the stout Duchess of Teck, Queen Mary's mother, his duty being to walk behind her when she went abroad, carrying her par-asol and bag. Then he grew older and taller and eventually came to work for my father. He was always very amiable to us children, remaining totally unruffled when we rushed upon him as he carried the coffee tray into the drawing room or the Saloon, to make a dive for the coffee sugar.

It was Cooper's job to dole out to us our one shilling a month pocket money. When the first day of the month came, we would hurtle downstairs and spring upon him, begging for our money.

'All right, Miss,' he would always say, 'Plenty of time.' He also put out the offertory for us on Sunday, one shilling each for the children; ten shillings for my mother.

Cooper was like the keystone of Kingston Lacy. Daphne and I were furious with our mother once when he went on holiday and was temporarily replaced by a very smart, professional parlour maid called Ling. Our mother had said that Ling was just as good and well-trained as the butler, which was horribly disloyal and ungrateful.

Mr Cooper was tall and dignified in appearance like the eminent statesman Lord Morley, with a long face and an aristocratic nose. We children thought he used to pronounce a soft, scarcely heard 'l' in 'could' and 'would', which perhaps was a feature of the dialect of Corfe Castle village where he had a small property. We used to have long talks with him whilst waiting for our mother to appear for her drive in the carriage or car. He was very discreet and would never tell us anything about our mother's guests.

'Who's coming tonight, Mr Cooper?' we would ask.

'Mr Kiffofflika', he would reply.

When we asked him if he had heard what we had been talking about at lunch, he would say, 'No, Miss. Too busy to listen.'

While we waited for our mother, Cooper would stand just inside the door, never showing the slightest sign of impatience but occasionally blinking his violet eyes slowly, like the wise old owl he was.

'Yes, m'. No m'.' he always said to whatever my mother told him to do or not to do. He was so well trained that if she had suddenly said, 'Go away and don't come back!', he would still have replied, respectfully and completely imperturbably, 'Very good m'.'

Cooper's relationship with the men who worked outside the house was very amicable. He would be a frequent visitor at many of the cottages in the village on his day off. On hot days, he would pause in his cleaning of the huge Charles II silver bowl, the silver Charles II Corfe Castle Mayor's mace or the silver cutlery in the butler's pantry to hand a bottle of beer through the open window to the gardeners toiling in the flower beds outside. He was, of course, an authority on all the wine in the cellars beyond the Servants' Hall, and was especially proud of the pipes of port and the champagne laid down at Ralph's birth.

So well trained was Cooper that he remained totally self-controlled on one of the few occasions in later years when even my mother's otherwise unbroken tolerance of anything Ralph might do suddenly snapped. Ralph, who had a Zenith motor bike with a powerful V8 engine, had been taking Cooper for a trip to his house in Corfe Castle. Driving too fast, he had had a collision with a car whose driver was equally uncertain which side of the road he should be on. There was immense local excitement. The villagers talked of how the young squire had only just survived, though it was Cooper who had been quite seriously hurt and who had ended up for a time in Wimborne Hospital. The words which Mama addressed to Ralph about the accident surprised us all by their vehemence, yet Cooper, the victim, breathed not one word of criticism or reproach.

Cooper and I had a special affinity and I found him a wise counsellor. Once, in London, hearing me on the telephone modestly making an invitation sound unattractive, he said quietly, 'Never cry stinking fish, Miss!'

Only Cooper and I genuinely delighted in showing off the Bankes collection of pictures to visitors, for example, the sublime *Judgment of Solomon* painted by Giorgione and Sebastiano del Piombo and the glorious Rubens of the Marchesa Brignole Spinola in, as we thought, a beautiful primrose bridal dress which turned out to be cream-coloured when the picture was cleaned. The Vandycks included portraits of Charles I and Henrietta Maria and a portrait of their children, the future Charles II, James II and the Princess of Orange, which had been given to Sir John Bankes of Corfe Castle by King Charles I himself. As a young woman I sometimes unexpectedly came across Mr Cooper in the National Gallery in London, though I never met Mama, Daphne or Ralph there.

Cooper lived on at Kingston Lacy for some years after my brother had returned there for good and the rest of us had gone. In his last days, he retired to his house in Corfe Castle and could be seen with a white beard, sitting outside in the sun.

Nothing ever went wrong with the smooth running of the household during the time that Cooper was our butler. He was as solid and reliable as the Bank of England and made Kingston Lacy seem just as secure. He slept in a comfortable room below the marble stairs next to the muniment room where a page from a Saxon Bible was found by the National Trust, and near a cellar where the silver was kept. Beside him lay a long, inlaid ivory revolver which his mother had given him.

Burglars were never considered such a problem at Kingston Lacy. There was always a night watchman who sheltered in a sentry box at the side entrance and occasionally wandered round the outside of the house. Until the National Trust took over there were no alarms of any kind, except for a row of bells, like sheep bells, hung on the inside of the shutters in the library which would have rung had a burglar obligingly pushed up the window and climbed in from the terrace.

The only time any notable incident occurred was after my brother was grown up. Looking out of the window one night, and not recognising the silvery form of the watchman making his way to the woods in the moonlight, Ralph seized his gun and shot at him. Fortunately, despite his usual deadly accuracy when shooting pheasants, Ralph missed. When a real burglar came, cutting a triangular section out of the front door and stepping in through it, Ralph, in the audit room, heard him on the marble staircase but thought it was Daphne. All the beautiful Tudor and Stuart miniatures, including some by Nicholas Hilliard, were removed. The thief had cut them all out of their little oval frames, some jewelled and very recognisable, which he had left in neat rows on the mat.

All the housemaids were very indulgent with us, especially when our mother was away, and let us play with them and slide on the newly polished floor which we were never allowed to do when she was there. I climbed on Edith's strong, broad back whenever she was on all fours dusting the oak boards, which cannot have helped her in her work. Kate, the Scottish head housemaid and eventually our mother's personal maid, was even more popular with us, even if she did rush menacingly along with a duster demanding to know, 'Who done it?' every time anything was broken, – apparently more interested in unearthing the culprit than about whether or not whatever it was could be mended or wiped up.

The nursery maids also relaxed in Mama's absence. Winnie, most spirited of all, even ventured to drop the 'Miss' when we were alone. Later on, she was to become our lady's maid and accompany us on our periodical, protracted educational visits to Paris with our mother. Dorset born and bred, she laughed so much at the strange sounds that she never learned a single word of French. She staunchly protected us from the dangers that she believed threatened two English girls abroad, though on her one visit with us to the *'Folies Bergere'*, blushing deeply, she left us to appreciate the strange spectacle alone. From the early days in the nursery to our 'Coming Out' in London she remained a firm friend. Then the inevitable happened, she too married a footman and disappeared from our lives.

(*Above*) My father, Walter
Ralph Bankes, at Kingston
Lacy in about 1900.

My mother, Henrietta Jenny
Bankes, shortly after her
marriage in 1895.

The south front of Kingston Lacy

(Opposite page) A rather
unlikely studio portrait of
Daphne and I, dressed as for a
holiday at Studland.

(Below) Studland Manor, now
a hotel, but where we once
spent many summers as
children.

Me, aged seventeen.

7
Art, Illnesses and Apparitions

When Daphne, Ralph and I were young the nursery and school room suite often became a children's hospital. There was always a trained nurse in residence for Ralph. Irish Nurse Collins followed Nurse Startin, then Jewish Nurse Levy was rushed from London when we had chicken pox, the local doctor from Wimborne lamenting that it was a 'great responsibility' looking after us. Chicken pox gave way to measles, then scarlet fever, diphtheria and whooping cough. Ralph even managed to acquire conjunctivitis after being sneezed over by an elephant in the zoo.

In the nursery, the principal remedy was what we called 'Blue Magnesia', because it was kept in a bottle wrapped round with blue paper to keep out the light. It was a clear liquid of no taste or use, but, perhaps it occasionally healed by suggestion. The detested castor oil was found in every nursery cupboard then. For bruises, we had a sweet smelling ointment in a small shapely jar called 'Pommade Divine', shortened to 'ma-divine' by us. When styes, boils and abcesses lodged with us, probably because we were over-fed, we would wander down to the kitchen where little Jinky would whisk up a frothy, yellow liquid made from brewer's yeast.

'Barm, barm, Miss.' she would call as we gulped the horrid mixture.

A wind-up phonograph was passed between sick rooms, Ralph's room always being first on the list, of course. It played a gay little tune which cheered us all up:

I'm all right!
She's all right!
Tra la la la la la la la la.

The governess and nurse would pick wild flowers for us when out on their walks and bring them to our bedside; snowdrops from the Lady's Walk during our winter bouts of influenza and lilies of the valley when the fresh spring breezes blew in a fresh batch of coughs, sneezes and raging temperatures. The maids, coming in to tidy our rooms and make up our fires, would ask with kindly concern:

'Are you feeling better, Miss?'

Nevertheless, we were still bored, tossing off our sticky bedclothes as soon as their backs were turned. It was a welcome distraction when our mother came to visit us, in moments gleaned from her busy life of farm and estate management.

I remember her also, in her London house, bending over my bed in her widows' weeds, bewitching pointed black bonnet and crèpe veil, when, at the age of five or six, I lay miserable and bed-bound after a tonsillectomy. It was then popularly believed that tonsils were best removed, being a focal point of infection. Whether it was necessary or not, it was certainly a nightmare experience.

It was the surgeon himself who placed over my face a mask attached to a black rubber football of gas, which he squeezed rhythmically. I tugged at his arm, convinced that I could not breathe. I did not know the very real danger there must have been of his not quite striking the happy medium between enough gas and enough oxygen.

Had I been a soldier, a century earlier, I might have been given alcohol, after surgery, to make me oblivious of the pain, and in 1905, laudanum was available. I was given no analgesics of any kind, however, since post-operative discomfort was taken as a matter of course. The tiny spoonfuls of ice cream which the nurse tempted me to swallow seared my sore throat like balls of fire.

My mother was very kind and sympathetic to me then. She was not so understanding on the occasion of Ralph's first serious accident. She had rented a house called 'Beech-field' one summer, so as to be near Nurse Startin's nursing home in Bournemouth fearing that Ralph might be ill. She was right. Her provoking son slid down the banister of the high staircase on his tummy, onto the stone floor, breaking his arm in three places.

'Are you going to break your other arm too, and break my heart?' she demanded of the unfortunate invalid.

An amputation was advised but Mama withheld her permission. Luckily, she knew a brilliant surgeon, William Arbuthnot Lane, who later became a baronet when he operated successfully on a princess of the Royal House. He had operated on the current Lord Nelson's nephew in the Trafalgar ward of Guy's hospital in his lordship's presence. Doctors from all over the world converged on the operating theatres at Guy's and at Great Ormond Street Children's Hospital to watch his quick, dextrous technique, rushing away to copy it, often with disastrous results. It was partly his methods of close observation and deduction, as well as those of Dr Bell of Edinburgh, that Sir Arthur Conan Doyle drew on in his creation of that most observant and logical of detectives, Sherlock Holmes.

Sir Arbuthnot himself was a gentle, amiable, quietly-spoken man with fearless, steel grey eyes. He performed operations on fractures which other doctors treated cautiously, though often very inadequately, without surgery. Fortunately, Sir Arbuthnot was one of the first surgeons to insist on the use of sterile caps, masks and gowns and pioneered a 'no touch' technique, using long-handled instruments. Though it was stiff for years, Ralph's arm healed beautifully. He wore a laced leather and steel support and had continual massage, but he still managed to learn the violin and his playing was almost faultless. The gardeners were ordered to teach him to dig to strengthen the weak arm muscles. In time he became a competent horseman and a good shot.

Mama henceforth worshipped Sir Arbuthnot. No wonder then, that when I was thirteen, he was trusted to remove my appendix. Was this preventive surgery too? It is true that I had had one or two slight stomach pains. On the other hand, appendicitis or 'peritiflitis' was a fashionable complaint with the smart set. Had not the King had to postpone his coronation because of it?

I did not spoil Sir Arbuthnot's good record. Though I experienced some post-operative pain and had to wear a leather and steel belt for years, I soon recovered and there were magnificent compensations at the time. In the London nursing home, I acquired a taste for Ovaltine, which I had never come across before, and my reluctant appetite was coaxed back into life by the most delicious fish soufflés.

Whilst recovering I received a complimentary and chivalrous letter from the universally feared head gardener, in which he quoted the lines,

    O Woman in her hours of Ease,
    Uncertain, coy and hard to please,
    When pain and anguish wring the brow,
    A ministering angel thou!

Not only did I ride all the way home to Dorset from London in an ambulance, but also, once at Kingston Lacy, in order that I would not have to be continually carried up and down four flights of stairs, I was ensconced on the first floor in my mother's room which had been my father's, off the hitherto forbidden marble staircase, installed by William John Bankes in the 19th century.

My mother's room, which had its own bathroom, was convenient because it was part of a suite of rooms which included the Saloon with its spectacular collection of sixteenth and seventeenth century pictures, the panelled dining room and the Spanish Room. The Spanish Room had been beautifully adorned by William John. Its walls were covered with golden brown Cordova leather and the entire ceiling, richly gilt and painted by Paul Veronese and Pordenone, had been removed from the Contarini Palace in Venice. On either side of the fire place panels of coloured marble in natural state were carved to look like fruit. Here, as in my mother's bedroom, the doors were painted with flowers, birds and animals.

William John, of immense wealth and owner of two estates, Kingston Lacy and Soughton Hall in Flintshire, was known in London as 'The Great Traveller'. He is reputed to have entered the Great Pyramid, and been the first European to enter the city of Mecca and come out alive. He had dressed as an Arab and pretended to be insane because Arabs were merciful to madmen, believing them to be special favourites of Allah.

William John was an *aide-de-camp* to the Duke of Wellington in the Peninsular War and, like many other officers, took the opportunity of conquest and pillage to acquire a large number of paintings. One day, the Duke of Wellington gathered his officers round a table and said: 'Gentlemen, the next man who is caught looting will be hanged' and, turning to William John added, 'And this goes for you too, Bankes.'

Wellington himself had captured a coachload of Joseph

Buonaparte's looted Spanish pictures.

The pictures in our Spanish Room included a Velasquez portrait of Cardinal Camillo Massimi and long, full-length pictures of Santa Justa and Santa Teresa by Zurbaran, which began to blister in the sunlight pouring through the large windows facing the front entrance.

William John, known as 'father of all mischiefs' when a fellow student with Byron at Trinity College, Cambridge, was a brilliant conversationalist as well as intelligent and good-looking. He was also a homosexual, and was banished from England following an unfortunate incident with a guardsman. He was allowed to return only on Sundays 'between sunrise and sun down', an ancient indulgence granted to Catholics in old Catholic England so that they could hear Mass on Sunday, temporal punishment not being allowed to interfere with spiritual salvation. Legend has it that Willian John took advantage of this concession to land from his yacht on his estate at Studland Bay and supervise the unloading of more works of art for Kingston Lacy. His lawyer brother, George, then living in the house, was worried by the enormous bills he had to pay for the treasures and was not so appreciative.

After I returned to Kingston Lacy without my appendix, I exulted in my sumptuous surroundings. Since it was considered dangerous for me to stand, I was conveyed everywhere in a cane seated, wooden carrying chair with handles fore and aft, like a sedan chair without a roof, by Ernest Masters, a footman, and Fred Pope, the Odd Man. My mother and I slept together in the great four poster, as if we were two of the six countesses who slept in the Great Bed of Ware.

All the servants were sympathetic and kind, but when Ralph later nearly died of appendicitis, nobody on the estate could talk of anything else.

'The young Squire's not expected to live!' they whispered to each other. Our mother was very grateful for their concern and when Fred Pope said: 'Excuse me 'm. Is the young squire better?', she raised his wages by five shillings a week. The church bells pealed out for Ralph's recovery, just as they had done for his birth.

The servants received very different treatment when they were ill. Usually their sufferings passed unnoticed, they themselves being too modest and too loyal to our mother to mention them. Just as our nurserymaid, Alice, had died of neglected appendicitis, so Beatrice Christopher, a third housemaid, was, much too late, discovered to have tuberculosis.

*　　*　　*

When I was older, my mother allowed me to sleep in the Red Room, so-called because of its red walls. Its large windows overlooked the obelisk and it had its own bathroom and dressing room. One night, not being able to sleep, I felt my way down flights of marble stairs in complete darkness into my mother's room. Suddenly jerked awake, she grasped the truncheon which hung at the side of the bed, fully prepared to beat me over the head with it, until she saw it was me and not a burglar, and invited me into the warm bed instead.

Throughout my life, the only thought that has ever terrified me has been that I might see a ghost. This fear orginated in early chilhood, when one of my mother's friends, Major Kenny Herbert, who had lost an arm in battle, told us a harrowing story.

At a house-party, a guest had boasted that he was not afraid of ghosts and refused to believe in them. That night, one of the other guests waited until everyone was asleep, took a gun and, having dressed himself in a sheet, invaded the boaster's bedroom. He stood at the head of the bed and made a noise, at which the boaster sat up and obstinately affirmed, 'I don't believe you're a ghost. I'm not afraid of you.'

The 'ghost' took his arm out of the white sheet and fired a blank cartridge three times. At the third shot, the boaster lay dead, of shock.

This story had led to much conversation at our dinner table about how there really were such things as apparitions. I subsequently lived in dread of them and, just before my final exile from Kingston Lacy, a ghost appeared.

In the seventeenth century the Duke of Ormond had died in the house after fighting a duel in the panelled dining room. But he had slept in the Red Room. One night, a tall, white figure in long white cere-cloths,, who could have been the Duke's ghost, appeared at the side of my bed, again an ancient four poster which the Duke himself might at one time have occupied. He pointed to the window, as if to say, only too prophetically,

'You will never sleep here again.'

I dived under the bedclothes in a cold perspiration, trembling with terror, the covers over my head. When I emerged about quarter of an hour later, the apparition had vanished.

8

Royalty

King Edward VII's visit to Kingston Lacy in 1905 meant endless preparation with the Governess in the school room. Even so, Daphne and I had not mastered the art of the graceful curtsey by the time he arrived. My mother received him on the steps of the porch, according to protocol. Inside the hall, the butler and footman standing by in livery and powdered hair, she introduced her three childen.

'One-two-three, bob!' she hissed at me loudly when it was my turn. Even at five years old, I knew that fine ladies were not usually so stage managed. The jerky, tearful parody of a curtsey which resulted produced a hearty royal guffaw which did nothing for my self-esteem.

The broad, white-bearded figure of the King had been driven past the country crowds lining the lanes from near-by Crichel, built for Sir William Napier in 1742, the home of Lord and Lady Alington with whom the King was staying. Near the house stood the White Farm, a plaything of Lady Alington. On its peacocks, as well as its hens, pigs, cart-horses, cows or pigeons, not a speck of colour was tolerated. All must be immaculately white. Lady Feodorovna Alington, on the other hand, daughter of the sixth Earl of Hardwick, was a dark, magnetic, Edwardian beauty, who greatly de-lighted the King. Her husband, Humphrey, Lord Alington, a stout man, heavy in walk and talk and not fond of chil-dren, laid on excellent shooting parties for his monarch on the downs.

Yet even a king is subject to ordinary afflictions. Just

before he visited us, he had sprained his ankle in a rabbit hole. For the ceremony of the planting of the cedar of Lebanon (only reigning monarchs were allowed to plant cedars at Kingston Lacy) his portly person was conveyed over the green lawn from the terrace steps to the tree in a pony chaise drawn by my pony, 'Silvertail,' my mother walking beside. Quite uncharacteristically, but fortunately for the dignity of the occasion – the tenants having been allowed onto the lawn to watch – 'Silvertail' was on her best behaviour. For many years, his majesty's cedar seemed sickly and stunted, then suddenly flourished and grew into a sturdy tree.

King Edward managed to hobble round the house to look at all our treasures, laughingly declining to honour an I.O.U. of £600 made by Charles I to his faithful subject and our ancestor, Sir John Bankes. We showed him Charles I's private brand on the back of a *Holy Family* by Raphael, which Charles I had also given to Sir John. In a glass topped table we kept a miniature of Byron and a signet ring and lock of Bryon's hair which the dying poet had sent to his friend, William John Bankes. Years later, when we were all grown up, the ring 'vanished' while some 'friends of friends' were looking round the house.

His majesty obviously enjoyed himself. He, the Alingtons and the Royal Suite were given tea in the panelled dining room with the Brussels carpet. The only disappointment for my ambitious mother was that the King refused to pose on the terrace for the customary photoraph with the family. We children never saw him again but, five years later, in 1910, in our grey mourning coats and dresses, highly polished button boots, we travelled up to London for his funeral. From specially reserved seats in the windows of the German Embassy, we watched the procession pass down the Mall, the coffin followed by Caesar, the King's wire terrier, and by the King's black charger with his majesty's boots turned the wrong way in the stirrups.

Two years followed Edward VII's visit before, in 1907, another cedar was planted at Kingston Lacy, by the Kaiser, during his Imperial visit to England. We were all to have new clothes for the occasion and Daphne and I were given huge white hats resplendent with curling, white ostrich plumes. Once again I was very shy and overcome by the occasion, though, in the photograph which Mr Pottle, the photographer, was allowed to take on this occasion, Ralph looks very perky in his white coat, white gaiters and white cloth cap. The photograph shows the Kaiser holding a cigar in his right hand. The other hand is invisible beneath his black Inverness cape, for it had been withered and useless since birth. While he was with us, he always kept his left hand in his pocket. On ceremonial occasions, when he dressed in the full uniform of a commander-in-chief, he would rest the withered hand on the convenient sword hilt.

We were all so captivated by the Kaiser's personality that we became very pro-German until the war, as did all the inhabitants of the towns and villages he passed through on his way to and from Highcliffe Castle where he was staying with General Stuart Wortley. He saluted indefatigably as grown ups waved and children threw flowers at his car. There were occasional undercurrents:

'I see you are prepared for the German invasion!' he said, jokingly, when he saw the row of cannon from my father's yacht along the edge of the lawn.

The Kaiser stared constantly at my beautiful mother who charmed him in fluent German. He talked to no one else, which suited Daphne and me. We were content to admire him from afar and watch his equerry peel him a ripe Kingston Lacy pear.

After the Kaiser left, he sent my mother a small terracotta bust of himself, made in his factory at Potsdam. It was rather out of place amongst the marble and bronzes of Kingston Lacy so it was placed in an inglorious corner of the Saloon. My mother gave him an engraving of Romney's *Mrs Bankes* by Scott Bridgwater and a specially bound and decorated set of Thomas Hardy. The Kaiser loved parcels and surprises so my mother's gifts to him were hung on the Christmas tree at his family party.

One day, at her house in Wilton Crescent, Mama was having tea with two German attachés when the double doors opened and Mr Cooper showed in the Kaiser.

'Ah!' he said, smiling and shaking his finger, 'You invite my attachés and you do not invite me!'

He wanted my mother to visit Berlin and to stay in the smartest hotel, the Hotel Adlon, in which he had shares. The visit never materialised. In any case, what would have been the Kaiser's reaction had he known that my charming and exquisite mother had intended to take Daphne and me with her?

There was renewed excitement in 1908 when news leaked out that the Princess of Wales, formerly Princess Mary of Teck, the future Queen of England, was coming to lunch. It was another dramatic responsibility for Jinky. Ralph, the silent, must be brought home from school in Bournemouth and made to be sociable, and Daphne and I could again wear our huge hats with the ostrich plumes.

The Princess was staying with the Shaftesburys who lived near us at Wimborne St Giles and hunted with the Portman hounds when they met at Kingston Lacy. I discovered later, when I too went hunting, how convenient it was to have Lord Shaftesbury in front of me, since he often inadvertently crashed down the hedges so that one could just ride through instead of jumping over. Lady Shaftesbury, who was very gracious and friendly, was entertaining a large party, most of whom accompanied the Princess when she came to luncheon.

I can still picture the Princess of Wales standing on the marble stairs with her elderly lady in waiting, just outside the door of the library, for she suddenly turned and, in an amazingly deep voice for such a young woman, and sounding very German, asked blushing me to hold the royal jewel case which travelled everywhere with her. It was a small, navy blue leather portmanteau with a gold fastening, and I regarded her request as a great honour.

At lunch in the dining room with its windows looking out onto the obelisk, the young squire in his white shirt, white jacket, white knee-length trousers and white stockings sat at the round table with our mother and the important guests, while Daphne and I, with due regard for our more inferior status, sat at a humble side table with the governess.

Daphne and I came into prominence again after lunch. Captivated by my angelic appearance, all in white with shining ringlets, the Princess patted me on the shoulder, and asked, in her almost sepulchrally deep voice,

'Are you always as good as you look?' – an impossible question for a child to answer. I turned fiery red, silently shifting from one foot to the other. My mother, who suffered from no inhibitions whatsoever and could be painfully outspoken, replied for me;

'No! This,' she said, indicating poor Daphne who immediately blushed too, 'is the good one.' My magnificent moment was over. The Princess, smiling kindly, turned away. Years later, when she was Queen, I wrote to ask her whether she would like to call on my husband and me at our Queen Anne house near Cambridge on one of her frequent visits to an antique shop in the city. A reply came that she 'could not accept my suggestion' but that she remembered me perfectly.

Daphne, Ralph and I stayed at home while the grown up party, in a stately procession of shining limousines, set out for Corfe Castle. We often went there ourselves for picnics, sailing through the gate as it was flung open by Bavistock, the keeper, an ex-army man, without having to pay our sixpences like the general public.

Little Prince Edward, the future King Edward VIII, had had to research the history of the castle for his mother and to write her an essay on the subject.

'Poor boy!' we thought, 'There is so much of it, even if you do leave out the few dull owners who did not inflict death or torture upon anyone, or suffer themselves.'

The castle had been called 'Corfe Gate' by the Saxons because it stood on a steep mound in a break in the Purbeck Hills. Here, in 978, beautiful Elfrida of Devon, who had inherited the castle from her husband, King Edgar, committed its first recorded foul murder. Wishing her own six year old son, Aethelred the Unready, on the throne, instead of Edward, son of King Edgar by a previous marriage, she had Edward stabbed in the back while he sat on his horse at the castle gate drinking the stirrup cup she had just handed him. Edward spurred away but died as he rode and toppled off his saddle, his body being dragged to the stream at the bottom of the hill.

Edward's corpse was concealed by the Queen and her servants at the bottom of a well for a whole year until it was discovered and reburied. Good King Edward had been very popular. He had supported saints Dunstan, Ethelwold and Oswald in their monastic reforms and, when miracles took place by his tomb, he was given the title of Martyr.

During the reign of King John twenty-two French knights were starved to death beneath Corfe Castle banqueting hall. As a punishment for foretelling the year in which the tyrant would lose his crown, a holy hermit, Peter of Pomfret, was dragged behind horses through the streets of Wareham and back to Corfe, where he was hanged on a gibbet with his son.

Edward II was a prisoner in grim Corfe before his merciless death at Berkeley Castle, and George, Duke of Clarence, who was an owner of Corfe Castle, was drowned in a butt of malmsey as Shakespeare records in *Richard III*. The castle was briefly occupied by the charitable, pious mother of Henry VII, Lady Margaret Beaufort, who endowed many schools and universities. Then it remained unappropriated until granted in fee by Elizabeth to her courtly favourite, Sir Christopher Hatton. Cannon were then mounted on its walls against the expected Spanish Armada, and Elizabeth granted the local people the right of returning two members to Parliament.

The connection of our family with Corfe Castle began in 1634, when Sir John Bankes, Attorney General, Chief Justice of the Common Pleas and one of King Charles I's Privy Council, in spite of its forbidding, fortress-like appearance and even more forbidding history, bought it for a family home. He furnished it with silks, rich tapestries and pictures, but though he made it comfortable, its sinister saga continued.

While Sir John Bankes remained with Charles I at Oxford during the Civil War, his wife, Lady Mary (whose bronze statue stands at the foot of the marble staircase at Kingston Lacy) and his six children, were beseiged in the castle by

Parliament. She and her few retainers held out for a whole summer, pouring hot coals down onto the heads of the soldiers as they attempted to scale the walls to hurl 'wild fire' over the battlements. Then Sir John returned to protect his family. Unfortunately, the following year, in 1644, he died and the castle was besieged again. This time, a traitor from within opened the postern gate.

In 1660, to replace their castle, the Bankes family had built Kingston Lacy on the site of an earlier house which having once belonged to the crown had come by marriage to a son of John Lacy, Earl of Lincoln. Beside the fireplace in the library, hung the huge iron keys and the round red seals of Corfe Castle which, admiring 'Brave Dame Mary's' spirit, Colonel Bingham who had commanded the final siege, had allowed her to keep. She and her children rode unhindered out of the castle gates in a carriage and six, taking with them many of the precious pictures which now hang at Kingston Lacy. Corfe Castle was partially demolished by Cromwell's forces and looted, many of its treasures ending up in the houses of the local gentry who, incredibly, refused to return them to the Bankes family, although Charles II restored the ruins to the heir, Sir Ralph Bankes.

When the Princess of Wales visited the Castle in 1908, she climbed the steep hill to the ruins with her friends and admired the impenetrable wall of ivy, said to be the oldest in England, which smothered the Norman keep. Historical curiosity satisfied, the elegant party descended the mound to the accompaniment of loud cheers from the crowd waiting in the old village of Corfe, where the upper storeys of the stone-roofed cottages jut out over the narrow paths. Opposite the rebuilt church, named after the martyred King Edward, on the other side of the stone cross in the market square where the ancient maypole used to stand, stood the Bankes Arms. Its stone porch had a small room over it like a miniature house, supported, above the pavement, by three stone pillars. There the carters used to sit drinking their cider. No doubt it was in a larger room of the inn that the Princess (on the recommendation of my mother who had wished to do the proprietor a service) ate one of the Bankes Arms famous lobster teas.

All that remained before the Princess left Kingston Lacy again was the planting ceremony. Not being a crowned monarch, she was not asked to plant a cedar. On this occasion my mother had chosen the more cheerful Liquidambar, a then quite rare tree with maple-like leaves that turn scarlet in the autumn. Like the cedars of Lebanon planted by King Edward and the Kaiser, the Liquidambar is still alive and blowing in the Dorset breeze today.

9
Studland Summers

How best to describe the halcyon months we children and the whole household spent every year in Studland Bay, the most idyllic corner of Ralph's estate? It seems they were always fine. Unbroken sunshine warmed the sand whilst the sea, shallow for a long way out, was warm, safe and perpetually inviting.

Whether we played tennis, dangerously practised unskilful archery or simply took tea in one of our airy, cliff top gardens, we never forgot the blue water stretching to the wide horizon under a clear sky, fringed on the right by chalk white cliffs curving out to the separate, stalwart column of Old Harry.

The sea was punctuated by minute, almost stationary brown or white dots of sailing boats and the bulkier forms of steamers, mesmerising us as we stopped to watch their steady passage, packed with tourists from Bournemouth, Poole and Swanage. Our own private path led first through a meadow, then steeply down, through brambles and straggling shadowy trees, to the beach that was, on one side, a wide open strand, on the other, cut into coves by the wooded clefts in the cliff.

The annual exodus from Kingston Lacy never failed to be exciting, particularly in the earliest days before our mother bought a car. The whole family and staff would assemble on the platform at Wimborne Station to wait for the heavy, hissing train of the London and South Western railway. We children, standing obediently beside the dignified figure of our mother, would cast longing glances towards the chattering servants who were grouped together at a respectful distance from us. Their activities seemed always so much more interesting than our own. Each of us clutched his or her green-covered *Answers* or orange brown *Titbits*, 'common' weeklies which, only on this one occasion and when we returned from our regular trips to the dentist at Bournemouth, were we allowed to buy and in which, once on the train, we ritually buried our faces as the journey to the coast began.

Comics were immediately discarded at Swanage. We sniffed the sea air outside the station, sensing our holiday beginning. Clopping in a local cab along narrow high-hedge lanes we were always delighted to overtake our own heavily-laden farm wagon with the two bay shire horses, or to negotiate the familiar hazard of Mr Behrens's cart pulled by his six donkeys. Our own riding and carriage horses would arrive later, trotting over from Kingston Lacy with Mr Crook and a groom.

All at once we would reach the top of the hill where Studland began. Through gaps in the hedge, over the fields, we would catch breathtaking glimpses of the wide coastline, the buildings of Bournemouth and Poole hazily discernible in the far distance over the bay, and nearer, Brownsea Island with its castle and woods, where probably, at that very moment, camped the Boy Scouts recently formed by Baden Powell.

While we waited for the lease of our mother's Dower House, the Manor, to expire, and the old tenant, deaf and dumb Miss Martin, to leave it, we successively occupied several houses, taking our choice, for all were on the Bankes estate. First, perched above Watery Lane, where even in the driest weather trickles of water found their way to the beach, was Cliff End, a ground floor villa which, together with the similar Wood End, our mother had built.

When we were at Cliff End, our mother, having her mind on matchmaking, even on holiday and even when we were ridiculously young, often invited the Bentincks, cousins of the Duke of Portland, to lunch. Freddy Bentinck, a trustee of the British Museum, would very endearingly throw back his head and laugh at our mother's jokes. We all liked him, with his friendly, red face, ginger hair and laughing blue eyes. We gazed with great respect at his wife, a militant suffragette and daughter of a gipsy, who had passed on her dark skin, hair and eyes to Barbara, her own daughter. It was Barbara on whom my mother's eye had alighted as a suitable wife for Ralph.

'Would you like to live in the country, my dear?' she inquired.

'No!' said Barbara emphatically.

Ralph, of course, never noticed Barbara at all. He warily stayed in the shelter of the grown ups to avoid the pinches of her then odious, later charming and ducal brother.

More splendid than Cliff End, at the Shell Bay side of Studland, was the roughcast Knoll House, now a luxurious, popular hotel, then a remote retreat in pine woods close to the sand dunes. When we ceased to need it, Knoll House was let on a long lease to the family of the Duke of Hamilton, all of whose children, including the eldest son, Lord Clydesdale, ran naked on the beach like little Cupids, or barefoot on the carpet of pine needles round the house. Sparton Nina, Duchess of Hamilton, obtained my mother's permission to replace the new-fangled indoor lavatories with back-to-nature earth closets in the garden.

The handsome thirteenth Duke of Hamilton and Brandon, black-haired and blue-eyed, had dived under a boat when young, hitting his head on the keel and damaging part of his brain, which affected his speech. We often encountered his suntanned figure, limping along the beach and waited, half in awe, half simmering with giggles, for his inevitable question about Ralph's health in which he was obsessively interested:

'How 'za boy? How 'za boy?'

'He's quite well thank you,' we would say, between suppressed squeaks of mirth, hurrying to catch up with our nurse. The lame Duke would watch us enviously, as we galloped on horseback over the wet sand.

Studland Manor, which eventually became our permanent holiday home, was closer to the village, at the top of the wooded cliffs overlooking the Bay and Old Harry. It had been built in 1830 but felt centuries older, with its dark oak beams and seventeeth century panelling, even after our mother had redecorated it. Predictably, it was said to be haunted, though no ghosts ever appeared to us.

Mama had built an enormous summer house in which, one day, we gave tea to Her Serene Highness, Princess Marie Louise Schleswig-Holstein. Thoroughly tired of entertaining royal visitors, Mama had thankfully informed Lord Malmesbury, with whom the Princess was staying, that she would be unable to show her the pictures at Kingston Lacy, as the whole household was moving to Studland for the summer.

'Never mind!' said his lordship, 'I'll bring the Princess to Studland instead!'

The peaceful garden of the Manor House, with its huge, old elm tree, its lawns, tennis court and superb view, was tended by a young gardener, John Horatio Savage, invariably seen in his wide, shady straw hat. There were four flower beds radiating from a central lead cherub, full of dark-red roses. On another lawn were beds of single flowered begonias, yellow and red and flat as saucers, and clumps of scarlet fuchsias whose buds popped very satisfyingly when, to our mother's fury, we squeezed them all.

John Horatio Savage was always very accommodating.

'Oh! Savage! Can you catch that spider in the summer house?' I would ask, 'it's sitting on my books and I don't like it.'

With a broad grin and a drawl more nasal than that of a backwoods Yankee, he would say, obligingly, 'Yes, Miss,' and take the offending spider carefully away.

In a trough of vile-smelling calcium carbide, in a long low shed, Savage produced acetylene gas, which gave a brighter light than came from ordinary gas. We would retch horribly as we peered in at him on our way to the kitchen. Savage did not mind the smell at all.

The shopping at Studland was all done by Loveless, a carrier and a bachelor as his name suggested. He called two or three times a week at the back door for our orders for Swanage. He was a most discerning shopper, charging us a halfpenny for each parcel carried. His old, good-tempered brown mare knew all the shops as well as he did, and stepped out eagerly to those which gave her sugar. She stood and waited endlessly for Loveless, who never found it necesary to tie her up.

Morning lessons with Miss Tidmarsh were relaxed and enthusiastic in the airy summer house. We studied with rapt curiosity the sea specimens we brought home: green lettuce-like weed which moved so beautifully with the sea's motion but which looked quite limp in a jar of tap water; a dainty, pink, fern-like seaweed; a few small crabs. In the night, with strange scuttlings like the scratching of long fingernails on polished wood, these newest recruits to

our collection left the jar to explore, startling Miss Tidmarsh as she sat alone, reading late by lamp light. She
ruthlessly removed them with a shovel and, too unnerved
to think of returning them to the sea, hurled them unceremoniously from the window.

Even when I could not do my sums, help was at hand.
Once I was forbidden to run down Watery Lane to the
beach with the others.

'You stay there until you've done your sums!' Miss Tidmarsh had said. She, Daphne and Ralph heartlessly de-
parted, leaving me solitary and in tears.

'I'll help you, Miss,' said kind Bessie Paine, the kitchen
maid, peeping through the door and coming to sit beside
me. Nobody ever found out how I earned the right to go to
the beach so soon.

One summer, we attentively watched our French governess, Madame Scotti, flirting madly with our straw-boatered
tutor Mr Gordon. He had been obtained by Mama from
Gabbitas and Thring to teach Ralph and three of his Day
School friends who were our guests. They were two
brothers, shy Guy Norrington, who always addressed me
lovingly as 'Old Sausage', and boisterous Pat Norrington,
and tiny Alaric Frampton (killed in the First World War)
with his pale, freckled face and two large front teeth, who
was enviably self-possessed when face to face with Mama.

The tutor was very stern when Pat tried to flirt too, putting
his arm around me and trying to get near enough too kiss.

'That will do! That's enough, Pat!' he would say firmly,
momentarily detatching his gaze from the fascinating governess.

We always had a trained nurse with us for Ralph, whose
health was a matter of permanent concern to our mother.
Nurse Da Costa, who wore a blue uniform and bonnet, was

Dutch and very pretty, with black hair and a little, tanned face. She was fond of Ralph and he of her. Daphne and I, however, were always irritated by the way she loudly called, 'Cis and Daphna!' – putting me first, though I was younger, and strangely mispronouncing Daphne's name. One day, we hid from her under the dark banisters, while she called and called:

'Cis and Daphna! Cis and Daphna! Vill you come, please!' When we came out of hiding, we were rather shame-faced to discover that she held a huge box of chocolates for us.

It was no wonder that, with such a large household of governesses, tutors and nurses, our mother would frequently decide that it was time to go to Marienbad for another 'cure.'

Except for Ralph's friends, the visitors at the Manor were mostly adults, the most charming probably being Lord Fisher, First Sea Lord of the Admiralty during the First World War, who used to waltz merrily with us on the lawn. Daphne and I would have liked friends of our own age to play with but we were quite good company for one another. Ralph, the self-contained, would not have cared if we had vanished into thin air, but he was always pleasant and sometimes affectionate and encouraging.

'Don't let yourself be beaten by an old tree,' he soundly advised when I was despondently thinking of abandoning my attempts to climb. He helped us to make a wigwam of odds and ends of branches torn down when mother was not looking and sat with us, pretending to enjoy the hot discomfort inside. Another day, he suddenly suggested 'a brolly battle'. We opened umbrellas and lunged at each other, till Ralph was victorious, his brolly piercing an enormous hole in mine.

Daphne and I, kept aloof at the command of Mama,

wistfully eyed the other children on the beach, who arrived in large numbers at Studland by wagonette and char-a-banc. One summer, in particular, we noticed the jolly, friendly-looking family of a Hatton Garden jeweller staying at the Bankes Arms. They played about near us, enticingly, but firm orders were given that we must not mix with them.

Fate, very mercifully, played into our hands. Escaping the dull beach tea-party of our nanny and governess one afternoon, Daphne and I climbed up the cliff through the tangly undergrowth for a game of hide and seek. I slipped on the loose chalk and, rapidly and helplessly, slithered all the way down, landing in a tearful, bramble-torn heap on the sand. The jeweller's children's nurse picked me up, splashed my hands and scratched legs with sea water and then tenderly bandaged them. After that, even our haughty Mama felt compelled to relax her ban.

There was always something enthralling to do at Studland that we could not have done at Kingston Lacy. If the fleet had anchored there, Ralph, owing to his inherited privilege as Lord High Admiral, granted by Elizabeth Ist, could have taken command. This never happened but we did have humbler and much more amenable craft at our disposal. Two boatmen, the Paine brothers, Albert and Gus, sons of white-haired old father Paine, who had a beard like Abraham Lincoln and spent his time gazing out to sea to forecast the weather, were detailed to look after us.

Albert, very polished and urbane, never seen without his smart, navy blue peaked cap, was proud of being yachtsman and steward to the Duke of Hamilton. Gus, by contrast, was cheerfully grubby and always in a dirty blue pullover and wide blue sailors' trousers. Each of the brothers would often take us quite far out to sea in a boat, then patiently sit back and let us row, giving just the odd tug or two on an oar to keep the craft straight.

Hitched behind our sailing dinghy when we went trawling, like the disciples in *The Calling of the Apostles Peter and Andrew* by Duccio, would be the round drag net. You never knew what would be in it when you hauled it up: crabs sometimes with shrimps in their mouths, small prawns, seaweed and flat fish tumbled out together in a glistening heap, so it was wise to keep fingers and toes out of the way. Once, to the outrage of the Kingston Lacy vicar's wife who was sailing with us, I perversely threw back into the sea a large plaice, without really knowing why. Another time, leaning over the edge of the boat to claw at some pink and green seaweed, I toppled right out, sinking, for one startled moment in the cold, deep water. I soon bobbed up, still wearing my big straw hat.

Large straw hats were always *de rigueur*, even for prawning round the rocks. For swimming, we changed inside our permanent bathing hut or moveable bathing tent into baggy full length costumes. Mine had been worn by my mother at Ostende and, at nine years old, I was proud to use it, with its dainty collar, trousers that came down to the ankles and sleeves to the wrists ending in frills. In a ritual beauty drill after a bathe, having hungrily devoured slices of ginger bread, we would smear our skin with stiff and sticky lanoline and cucumber to prevent freckles. While I would acquire a clear, golden tan, poor Daphne's fair face seemed, after each anointing, even more densely peppered with freckles than before.

The beach at Studland was divided by red sandstone rocks from which we scratched tiny chippings to mix with yellow and silvery tints of sand and arrange in layers in a jar. My sand pattern, like the flower arrangements we made, suspiciously earned First Prize in the local show.

On one side of the sandstone outcrop, the beach was quiet and safe for swimming. On the other the fishing boats were pulled up and turned upside down and there was a shop on the bank above where dapper, white-moustached Mr Walker, a great friend of Mr Cooper, sold cakes and tea. He plied Mr Cooper with jam puffs or huge, delicious fly biscuits from his village shop, while the butler, too dignified to plunge into the sea himself, perched on a rock to watch us swim.

One great sandstone rock, the height of a man, had a comfortable hollow in the middle into which we and our wire-haired terrier would climb to bask in the sun. One afternoon, I left behind in the hole a beautifully illustrated cloth-covered book belonging to Mama, the title of which, in gilt letters, was *Lillian's Golden Hours*. When I returned later and scrambled up to fetch it, it had vanished. In its place was a fine malacca cane with a silver band.

The village of Studland was secluded. A handful of thatched cottages, each with a pretty garden shaded by thickly foliaged trees, stood grouped round the Church of St Nicholas, patron saint of fishermen and sailors as well as of children. On Sunday mornings, from all our houses except Knoll House, which was too far away, we would hear the four large church bells chiming out, calling us to obey the inscription on the largest or tenor bell, 'Draw near to God.'

Mr Guppy, short and grey haired, with a beard like King Edward's, was the bell ringer. His face would be white and drenched with perspiration by the time we arrived from the effort of pulling the four ropes hanging against the wall a few feet from the pulpit. He would never have considered taking off his coat. The bells gave out beautiful sounds, the music changing every five minutes until a final, urgent,

'Hurry up or you'll be late!
Hurry up or you'll be late!'

The tune ended with one single note, after which Mr Guppy shut the cupboard containing the ropes and solemnly took his own place in the church.

Thanks to Mr Guppy, we were always on time, not forgetting to feed the importunate donkey who lived in the church yard and butted you in the back if you forgot his carrots.

The walls of St Nicholas Church reputedly dated from the seventh century, when St Aldhelm, according to a Saxon chronicler, 'built a church near Wareham by Corfe Castle, where the hills jut out to the sea.' There were grotesque carvings under the outside eaves, contorted animal and human figures beloved of swallows and house martins. Inside, I was always coaxed, at least for a moment or two, into an uncharacteristically solemn mood by the massive Norman arches, all the more impressive for being in a tiny, village church.

The Rector of Studland and of nearby Brownsea Island was the Reverend Frederick Swift Algeo, medium in height, with iron grey hair and moustache. He strode along the beach – none of it then reserved for naturists! – to officiate in the church on Brownsea every other Sunday. We thought him rather too intellectual a preacher for a village community as we grew older, and, when we were young, delighted in counting up the number of times he used the word 'supernatural' in the pulpit. He was much loved by all his parishioners, however, and would drawl 'Good morning, my friend,' or 'Good evening, my friend,' to all and sundry. His poor little pale-faced wife was very deaf and would hold out her ear trumpet to us so we could speak directly into her ear.

The Rector's son, Willy, used to explore the heathland with us. We found tadpoles in the many pools, looked for the rare blue gentians and lay on our faces to watch the fly-eating sundew plant which slowly closed over and absorbed the tiny pieces of raw meat which we dangled over it on black cotton. We often brought back wild ferns for our rockery, but invariably, they died.

When the Reverend Algeo was away, his place was taken by the Reverend Warner who lived at Combe House on the land left to my father's mistress, Elizabeth Marshall, and hastily bought back by my mother. Mr Warner was soft-voiced and retiring but always forgot his shyness in his eagerness to preach. Of course, Daphne and I never listened to his sermons, but he was so personable, with rosy cheeks and a deep tan, that we both fell deeply in love with him. We used to crane our necks round the stone Norman arch-way, so old that the joins no longer met, to catch his eye so that he blushed. How excited we were when we heard that he was coming to tea at the manor, and how disappointed when we learned that his wife and three children were coming too!

Studland was full of interesting characters, whether des-cendants of old Studland families who live there still, or visitors attracted there by its unspoilt natural beauty. We used to see, out on the cliffs with his easel and water colours, the Honourable John Collier, known as 'the problem painter', because no one could ever quite decide what the picture he exhibited each year in the Royal Academy was all about. Mad old Teddy Durham, in his horribly dirty clothes, would follow us a little way on our walks, taking off his cap and muttering frighteningly and unintelligibly after us.

In the grey stone house on top of the cliffs near Old

Harry, where my father had lived when he was a bachelor and went duck shooting on the moors, lived a retired, well-known Jewish professor of entomology, Albert Michael. Daphne and I and even Ralph were always help-less with hysterical giggles when Mr Michael spoke to us, in a bat-like voice, high and squeaky, eyeing our painfully straight faces very seriously from under his Panama hat.

Spiders at Studland were unusually large and apparently ferocious. Mr Michael, we thought, was just the person to tell us about our own captive spider, friend or relative of one which had bitten me in the night and left me with a red mark as it scuttled away. We put the match box containing the spider into the corner of Mr Michael's pew in church, and kept looking over our shoulders at him during the service, hoping that he would open it and jump with shock. Open it he did, but without the slightest flicker of surprise. He was used to insects in little boxes. He waited for us in the church porch and, in his thin high voice, gave us a long lecture on the spider's family and habits.

Our mother never came down onto the beach with us, for she was usually entertaining guests. She never relaxed her strict attitude toward her daughters. I once, unguardedly, called her 'clumsy Miss Mumsy' when she dropped some-thing and was severely scolded, though she seemed not to mind when her son and heir casually called her 'Marsy'. Daphne and I once discovered from an old album that it would soon be her birthday. When the day came, we went out early and searched for flowers: buttercups, camomile and sorrel, forget-me-nots, purple willow-herb and wild lupins, yellow flax, wild geranium and pink campion. The governess gave us a blue ribbon to tie them with and when our mother came out of her room at ten o'clock we handed her our little offering, smilingly wishing her 'Many happy returns!'

'Who told you?' she demanded angrily, snatching the flowers and flinging them out of the window. Daphne and I ran outside and shed shocked tears in the garden. We were in disgrace all day and the governess, privately scolded, remained equally silent and subdued.

We must have soon recovered from our disappointment. There was so much to occupy us. There were the Tilly Whim caves near Swanage to peer into. Reputedly made by smugglers, they were really part of a disused quarry which the quarry men maintained did not belong to the Bankes Estate because they were *under* the ground, not *on* it, and subject to no laws.

When we were little, we used to ride in the wagonette to the large, reddish-brown Agglestone Rock on the heath, an easy walk later. The devil, a notoriously bad shot, was said to have aimed it at Corfe Castle from Old Harry. Old Harry itself was out of bounds, for the tide came in so quickly over its shingled beach that people would often be cut off. One unhappy group of tourists had spent all one night on top of the single column of Old Harry, bravely keeping up their shivering spirits by singing the hymn *For those in Peril on the Sea*.

10

The Sporting Life

Although I was always an animal lover, it was impossible to live at Kingston Lacy without sampling the traditional amusements of hunting, shooting and fishing. I enjoyed putting white worms on a hook to catch roach and pike, and sitting long, pensive hours by the flowing river. It was also tremendously exciting to ride out on a winter's morning into the woods or onto the downs accompanied by the eerie, disturbing sound of the huntsman's horn.

My father had been a fine shot, though he had for a time, until cured by a Viennese doctor, lost the sight of one eye from a bullet that had glanced off a tree. I myself never mastered the art of shooting. When Boast, the gamekeeper, attempted to teach me I did not hold the heavy gun firmly enough. It kicked so hard that it nearly removed my front teeth, teeth which were already ridged from being 'cut' during scarlet fever and prone to attracting unsightly strands of spinach at lunch.

Riding was much more enjoyable. I was taught as a child and at first wore a bulky, voluminous habit laboriously put together by Mrs Lush in her cottage in the village. My riding steadily improved, though I never became an expert horsewoman with full control of my mount. When I was seventeen I had private horse jumping lessons in London, riding without a saddle to increase my confidence. These lessons soon stopped, for I despised the bowler-hatted, horsy instructor. His petty behaviour in the huge, sandy ring shocked and disgusted me. When his horse cantered up to a jump too quickly, then stopped dead, the instructor, who was trying to demonstrate to me how such a jump should be perfectly taken, flew over its head. Instead of brushing himself down and calmly remounting, unable to bear his loss of self respect, he was furious with his horse, slashing it horribly and unforgivably with his switch.

This was a far cry from our gentle rides at Kingston Lacy. We used to trot out with Mr Crook down the Blandford Drive and were soon enjoying the wind-swept solitude of Crichel downs, which joined the Bankes property. Our horses tossed their heads joyfully and loved the freedom of a canter over the soft turf, skilfully avoiding the hazardous honeycombs of rabbit burrows.

We often rode down the stately avenue of beech trees planted – for what reason nobody knows – by William John Bankes in 1835. There were 385 trees on one side and 386 on the other. The avenue led to Badbury Rings where we would trot round the immense, grass-covered circular ramparts, the outermost of which is a mile in circumference. The rings rise, one above the other, to a circular plateau where we picnicked and gazed over the misty Purbeck and Dorset hills while we munched Jinky's delicious paté sandwiches.

In my early twenties, and after Mr Crook had died ('loyal friend of the Bankes family at Kingston Lacy. Faithful unto death' as it says on his tombstone) a groom fed and looked after my horse. I saddled and bridled it myself. In my well-cut gaberdine riding habit, which had been expertly tailored for me in London, I would ride out to the Rings alone, putting myself mystically in touch with the primitive past. Daphne, whose figure became quite rounded as she grew older, did not think she looked her best in a riding habit and preferred to walk.

East Dorset was hunting country and any farmer who dared to put barbed wire on his fences was ostracised. The first meet of the New Year was always at Kingston Lacy, with Lord Portman, Master of Fox Hounds, presiding in his glossy silk hat. Ralph never attended it, though he usually went cubbing in September. At half past five in the morning, in the heavy damp mist he would shame his sisters by walking his horse very slowly onto the scene some twenty minutes late, with no explanation or apology, while everybody waited and hounds bayed to be off.

'Ralph, why are you so late?' I would demand, 'You've kept everybody waiting.'

'Oh, I don't think I was late,' he would reply, maddeningly.

The cubs were not killed but the huntsman noted the earths in preparation for hunting later and sometimes stopped one up.

Before the hunt began, horses, riders and hounds collected in a restless group in the main drive, excitement mounting, as friends who were going to follow on foot or in their cars, gathered round and the butler and footman handed out port wine and fruit cake. Then we set off.

The rules of the hunt were strict. I was not allowed to wear a top hat like that of the Master's wife, Lady Portman, but only my bowler. We were forbidden to call the hounds 'dogs', or to refer to their tails as anything but 'sterns'. Nor were we allowed to pat their heads, for we were firmly told that they were not to be considered as pets. Once, totally unable to control my spirited mount, I committed the sin of riding ahead of hounds, face flaming with shame, while a huntsman swore at me from behind the hedge.

I was used to riding both on the right and on the left of my saddle, partly as the result of being treated by a

Swedish masseur, in order to correct curvature of the spine, which I was said to have by Sir Arbuthnot Lane. When I rode astride, having no pommel to hold onto, I found it hard not to be dislodged. Usually I was hopeless at jumping, often falling, then having to brush mud off my riding skirt before struggling into the saddle again. A hunt could last for seven hours and was an endurance test for every rider. On one such hunt, every time I opened my little tin sandwich box, hoping to eat a sandwich or a piece of plum cake, the 'tally ho!' was given and I only just managed to close the box without dropping it before we were away.

My mother did not go hunting but followed us on her bicycle, which could sometimes be very inconvenient. For there was, in the neighbourhood, a certain Colonel Maddock, who had married a widow, Mrs Mason, with a desirable property just outside Wimborne. He was 'just looking for a house to hang his hat up in,' said Jinky. What a pity Mrs. Mason had not heeded the old rhyme, 'Change your name and not the letter; change for worse and not for better.' Colonel Maddock would come down early in the morning, the gossips said, and pinch the housemaids. My mother disapproved strongly of him. She had sent him a frosty note when she had looked out of the window one morning and seen him on his horse, taking a short cut to Badbury Rings across the park.

'I should be obliged if you would go round by the road in future,' Mama wrote.

'You must never ride with him, Cissie,' she told me sternly.

One or twice, unknown to anyone, the flirtatious Colonel Maddock and I met on the downs for a canter. It was not very exciting, particularly when I was silly enough to be talked into swopping my spirited horse for his stodgy old mare. Someone talked and the meetings stopped abruptly.

It was most irritating later, when, happening to exchange a few words with the Colonel as we chanced to ride close by each other during a hunt, I saw the flat, black cycling hat of my mother loom menacingly from behind a hedge.

11

Faith and Duty

We sat at the back of St Stephens's Church in the family pews beneath the window containing all the coats of arms connected with our family and its marriages. Our pews were raised higher than those of the rest of the congregation, mother and Ralph having joined oak arm chairs on one side of the aisle, and Daphne and I two exactly similar chairs on the other. There were also two raised rows at the back for our visitors and friends. In addition to fighting against being distracted by us, the Reverend Parry Evans could not fail to notice Mama, staring at her watch throughout his sermon, and looking extremely fierce if he dared to speak for a moment longer than his allotted ten minutes.

St Stephen's Church, up whose cream and brown walls climbed many shrubs and creepers, had been built of Portland stone in the Park by mother with money left for the purpose by my father in his will. It was truly a family church, though open to the villagers and under the authority of the Ecclesiastical Commission. One window showed us children gathered round the feet of Christ with the words 'Suffer little children to come to me.' Another window showed Ralph seated, as the Christ child, in the Temple. In a niche outside a statue of Saint Stephen stood with his hand on Ralph's shoulder, and a high stone cross had been erected as a memorial to our father. Into the design of a beautiful altar cloth for feast days were embroidered symbolic daphnes and violas, and roses for Ralph, interwoven with gems donated by Mama, Daphne and me. My own rather reluctant contribution had been a most precious and treasured amethyst necklace.

On Sunday mornings, Mama, Daphne, Ralph and I would walk up through the wood to the church along a private path, sometimes meeting tenants who, on just that one occasion each week, were allowed to take a short cut across the park. All the staff, indoors and out, would attend the service. From our lofty seats at the back, we had a good view of everybody: Tommy Gollop, the verger, with his son; Tom Shears, the head woodman; Mr Whiffin, a bricklayer turned postman; Percy Ricketts, the painter, and tall Iky Score from the Post Office, with his mother, 'Grannie' Score from Tolpuddle. The Haytors from the farm would be there with their son, Gerald, a pupil at Wimborne Grammar School. There was also Mr Marst, who eventually went to seek his fortune farming in New Zealand.

Mr P. J. Jacobs, the head clerk at the estate office, would not be visible, playing the organ, but Mr Hill, the head gardener, would be standing in front, solemnly wearing his silver chain across his chest. Mr Crook, the coachman, short and tubby, would fill the whole church with the smell of the camphor balls in which his wife stored his Sunday suit. We would also see Mr Ward with a white beard, who made our curtains (always a little too short), and Mr Budden, the blacksmith whom, on weekdays, we would stand and watch from the door of his forge, sometimes being allowed in to hammer the red hot iron ourselves.

The choir, many of whom also formed the Kingston Lacy football and cricket teams, was largely composed of estate workers and was very well trained, practising hard each Friday night. We children would always peer down the nave in horrified fascination to stare at one of the singers who worked at the estate saw mill and had accidentally sawn off all the fingers from one hand.

The church was always spotlessly clean. On the altar were always white arum lilies from our sunken green house at Kingston Lacy. They were only replaced on Whit Sunday by red geraniums, which grew thickly against the wall under the grey stone terrace. At Harvest Festival, immense quantities of fruit would appear, the villagers vying with one another in the production of outsize tomatoes, giant apples, swelling pumpkins and golden brown loaves of bread. After church, our mother would hold court in the porch, Daphne and I being as charming as we could to everybody, while Ralph stood in silence, waiting for us to walk back up to the house.

The Reverend Parry Evans, who had a good singing voice, was a most popular curate-in-charge before we had a vicar of our own. He was responsible to the vicar of Wimborne and said services every day in Wimborne Minster as part of his duties, though he was allowed to live in the small square rectory in Pamphill village. The Bankes had the gift of the living and could choose the incumbent, as we could at Shapwick and Studland, Parry Evans had been selected by mother for his Low Church views since she herself had had a strictly Presbyterian upbringing. Like Mr Hervey, he became a trustee during Ralph's minority and was very fatherly towards him, and a good companion, sharing his fondess for shooting, though not his skill. He and his wife, in her long skirts, would play tennis with us on our court beside the house. He was always very kind and only occasionally ecclesiastical:

'Cis! Cis!' he said reproachfully one day, when I exclaimed, 'Damn!', after sending a ball into the net with my fearsome, underarm serve. 'Surely, you know better than that!'

For a time, on winter Sunday evenings, a solemn procession would wend its way to St Stephen's Church from the house, with the whole household ranked in order of seniority. They were led by the swaying lantern held by the coachman, shakily illuminating the trunks of the old trees and the wondering, watching eyes of the wakeful Red Devon cattle. Mother, in her widowhood, had a religious phase and, at one point, was almost tempted to turn the billiard room into a chapel.

Probably the time we were closest of all to Mama was when we were very young and recited prayers at her knee. Sadly, she did not continue to pray with us for long and it was not until years later that I experienced any religious feeling. We all had specially bound and initialled prayer books and would sit obediently in church, following the service, but it was the personalities of the clerics whom we met, rather than their message, which impressed us.

Bishop Wordsworth of Salisbury, a very scholarly, noble figure, climbed heavily up the stairs to the schoolroom before breakfast when staying at Kingston Lacy, much to our surprise, to say prayers with Daphne and me and the governess, which provoked the customary suppressed nervous hysterics. We were tense with terror, lest the creaking William and Mary cane chair on which he sat should give way. He spoke very wisely and kindly to us, singling me out for an explanation of the symbolic significance of his colourful ecclesiastical rings, which, however, still seemed a little extravagant for a Christian leader.

Very different was Father Ignatius, frail and holy in soutane and white beard, the eighty-year-old resident priest in a secluded convent near Wimborne. He had entered the religious life as a boy and had never been known to speak to any woman other than the sisters, until my charming mother asked to meet him. She persuaded him to leave the sanctuary of his cell to visit us, an incongruous, apostolic figure amid the opulence of Kingston Lacy. After lunch he tottered round the huge Saloon on my mother's arm, gazing at the pictures with wonder and immense enjoyment.

The Bishop of London, Dr Winnington Ingram, also came to stay with us from Lambeth Palace. Daphne and I were very impressed by his pale, sensitive features and mystical eyes. Mama asked him to give our unenthusiastic 'delicate' brother a special blessing.

The last Bishop to visit us was Bishop Wordsworth's successor, Bishop Ridgeway. For once confused about etiquette, our mother hesitated about whom to place on her right at lunch, the bishop or Viscount Portman, who was also present. Most gallantly and correctly, Lord Portman said that of course a spiritual lord takes precedence over a temporal one. Once more Mama asked, and obtained, a special blessing for Ralph who, meanwhile, secretly observed by Daphne and me, continued eating grapes and spitting out the pips.

The proximity of Kingston Lacy to Wimborne meant that we frequently visited the minster with our governess. Possessing a church of our own, unlike the rest of the local 'quality', we did not worship regularly in the minster, though mother would sometimes be solemnly driven there in the brougham for a funeral.

From whichever side you approached it you could see the square towers of the minster, which was dedicated to the sister of Ina, King of the West Saxons, St Cuthberga, who had founded a Benedictine nunnery there in the early eighth century. There had once been a spire which had fallen during a service in 1602, miraculously without hurting anyone. On the outside of the bell tower, above the door by which you entered, was the Quarter Jack which, during the Napoleonic Wars, had changed from a monk to a colourful grenadier. We begged our governess to wait while we watched him strike his two bells at each quarter of an hour.

We never tired of exploring the minster. We loved to touch the heavy links on the ancient books in the chained library. The fourteenth century astronomical clock had not then been restored to its present bright colours but the gilded cherubs and angels already decorated it, having been taken from the old organ case and put there in Victorian times.

Like us, Charles Dickens had noted the name 'Snodgrass' on a small tablet in the minster, and there was, on the floor, a tombstone commemorating Isaac Gulliver, one of the most successful of all Dorset smugglers. We were fond of the seventeenth century monument to Sir Edmund Uvedale, with its two left feet, and Anthony Ettrick's coffin, oddly placed in a recess in a wall at his request to avoid breaking his own testy oath, sworn in a moment of anger towards the people of Wimborne, that 'he would never be buried within the church or without it – neither below the ground nor above it.'

Most interesting of all were the minster's connections with our family. One window showed the lives of four saints of Wessex, including King Edward the Martyr, murdered at Corfe Castle. There was also the burial vault of the Bankes family, for ever sealed after the last two men had been laid to rest there, William John Bankes in 1855 and my father, Walter Ralph, in 1904, with special permission from Parliament. Intramural burial is no longer allowed, since it is thought to be unhygienic. In the three lancets of the great east window, depicting the Line of David, was fifteenth century glass said to have been procured by William John

Bankes from a Belgian convent, though it was more probably looted by him in the Peninsular War.

Our mother knew all the dignitaries of the minster and took us to tea with Canon Hartdyke, a dear old man whose few remaining hairs blew in the wind. He was especially proud of his rockery. Very self-controlled and courteous, he pretended not to notice when Mama unluckily stepped on a precious rock plant which burst with a loud squelch.

It was not until the Second World War, when my husband was in the forces, that I understood how comforting faith can be. In childhood, we obediently observed the forms of religion, without question, like the Light Brigade, ours 'not to reason why'. Even when being prepared for our confirmation at eleven or twelve years of age, Daphne and I could not take the classes seriously. We were coached by the Reverend Thicknesse, a very serious gentleman who lived in Grosvenor St. and who looked solemn and glum by turns, as his cheerful Aberdeen terrier wagged its tail, 'Thump! thump! thump!' on the drawing room carpet.

I had a pretty, new frock for the ceremony but was afterwards unkindly told by the nursery maid that I had spoilt the effect by obsessively wiping my nose whilst I knelt at the altar.

The strain of endeavouring to please Mama was beginning to show.

12

Mama

'Now that your husband is dead, I suppose you'll marry again,' Nurse Stanley once said, impudently, to mother.

It was a measure of her unbalanced state that she realised neither the offence she gave (mother still remembered it years afterwards) nor the unlikelihood of her suggestion. Surrounded by all the advantages of wealth and independence, why should she risk pain and inconvenience a second time? Far safer to make the best of her situation as dutiful mother and capable business woman, while thoroughly enjoying the admiring and over-optimistic attentions of the local landlords. Still vivacious and beautiful, she also took full advantage of the opportunities Kingston Lacy afforded for entertaining the most interesting and eminent people.

The neighbouring landowner who courted her most assiduously was Lord Portman, top-hatted master of fox hounds, who had a great sense of fun, despite the sinister black shade he wore over one eye. He always sent her a haunch of venison during the annual deer cull. He would have been a very suitable husband to help Mama with the running of the estate, had she agreed to marry him, but she was determined to keep the Bankes and the Portman estates completely separate, so that Ralph's patrimony should be in no way endangered or joined to the Portman land.

Perhaps Colonel Nicholson, perpetual prospective Conservative candidate for East Dorset after a distinguished career in South Africa, might have been a more successful suitor, had my mother felt herself free to marry, since he was an even closer more deeply loved friend to all of us than Lord Portman. He was always out canvassing with his devoted chauffeur, Holland, who would wait for him in his open, four-seater car for hours. He was invariably optimistic, despite the traditional propensity of Dorset people to throw rotten eggs at candidates at political meetings, and despite the Guest iron fortune with which, it was rumoured, Cornelia Lady Wimborne who lived in Canford Manor, had gilded the way for her second son, Freddie Guest, to win the election for the Liberals.

We all staunchly supported the Colonel, and were extremely indignant about the continual Liberal successes. When the Colonel came on to us after a visit to Crichel, my mother indignantly tore out of his button hole the red carnation which Lady Alington had given him and flung it on the fire. Daphne and I were extremely unkind to the daughters of Fred Richards, our mother's tenant, who sometimes came to Bournemouth in the car with us for shopping and who had been very proud of their red Sunday coats.

'Of course, you're little Radicals, aren't you, with your red coats?' we taunted, in insulting whispers in the back seat.

The Colonel was always friendly towards us children, though the presents he gave us were bought not so much to please us as to ingratiate himself with his recalcitrant constituents. Prince Loti, our well-bred pedigree Pekinese, was the happy result of one of these transactions, though the unbroken, vicious pony he bestowed upon us for the same reason was, sensibly, restored to him without delay by Mama.

Colonel Nicholson would have been a very jolly stepfather for us, being a noted good sport. We could ask him ridiculous riddles or play jokes on him without the remotest fear of reprisals. Wet sponges would fall on his head; plates and spoons rise up and down before him on the table, without his good humour being in the least ruffled. At one of the annual village fêtes which mother allowed to be held in the grounds of Kingston Lacy, the Colonel sat inside a barrel, bobbing up now and again for people to try to knock off his top hat. He also helped Mama to establish a rifle range, with a reading room attached, for the local community. Not only did he indulge our childish sense of humour, but he also flattered us by often speaking to us in a very grown up way, bewilderingly accusing us of having 'cut' him when, busy trying to control our startled, plunging mounts, we had not acknowledged his wave from his speeding car.

Despite her many friends, Mama never ceased to take an interest in us as children. She had loved us dearly as babies and always kept, in a brocaded box which is still at Kingston Lacy, a long lace christening dress and three little bonnets marked with our names and dates of birth.

As we grew older, she saw us every day after tea and allowed us to sit quietly playing 'beggar my neighbour' behind her, so long as we did not talk while she was writing. When she was in a good mood, she would pedal away at the pianola fixed onto the drawing room piano, playing us songs such as 'Daisy, Daisy' and 'King Cotton's March' and tunes from the musical comedies of the time. When we learned to ride bicycles, she would cycle out with us, for the sake of her figure, in her perfectly flat black hat with a veil, along the avenue of trees towards Badbury Rings.

When we were in Mama's London house for the 'season'

it was a special treat to stay up in the evening to see her all ready to go out to a Court Ball at Buckingham Palace. Like Daphne and me, she would be tightly laced in a corset with a waist as small as possible, under her low cut black dress. She wore a diamond tiara which we thought very spectacular. At Kingston Lacy, her only jewellery would be a green malachite ring with the Bankes crest of a Moor's Head, which only families descended from Crusaders were allowed to wear, or sometimes a gold bracelet, gold watch and a string of pearls to which was attached a disturbing story.

Knowing that my father intended to buy her a betrothal present, Mama had gone by herself to a jeweller's in Bond Street the day before and made certain that she would be able to identify the best necklace in the shop. When she returned the next morning, as if for the first time, with Papa, they were met by the jeweller who helpfully asked, 'Did you wish to see the pearl necklace you chose yesterday, Madame?'

When she was in London, Mama enjoyed all that the city had to offer in the way of entertainment. She often took Daphne and me with her to the Russian opera, the Russian ballet, all the most notable concerts and even the Music Hall. At Covent Garden, we would sit right at the back of her box in the shadows, watching her bowing and waving to the people she knew, carrying on for our benefit a running commentary about the fashionable beauties of the day.

It was during her hours of estate management at Kingston Lacy that Mama was unapproachable. The architect was astonished at her understanding of the elevations on his drawings and the young estate agent, Alfred Lodder, would stand meekly and respectfully beside her, by the hour, making notes as she decided what should or should not be done about the farms and cottages. She had little diplomatic flair, preferring to sell the part of the estate at Holt, with the permission of the trustees, rather than cope with the complaints of the tenants about leaking roofs and drains.

Mama always worked at a mahogany, leather-topped, kneehole desk in the library, overlooking the terrace on the ground floor. She was surrounded by delicious-smelling books in old bindings, some dating from 1500 and some in manuscript form. I would sit quietly on the comfortable four-seater sofa, or in my father's old high-sided chair that kept the draught off, watching her writing, her brown hair caught into a bun at the nape of the neck. Her small, plump hands were smooth and white since she never did anything to dirty them, standing up only to ring the bell for the manservant when the fire needed coal or logs.

It never occurred to me to wonder whether she was happy. She would have thought it extremely vulgar to show any emotion. Did she ever remember the sister who had betrayed her by acting as a go-between for my father and his mistress? Did she still feel hurt that her brother, Jack Fraser, towards whose diplomatic career she had paid half her income before her marriage, had secretly married Ruth Vincent, a pretty musical comedy actress?

Mama was as strict with us as she was with herself. We soon learned that it was not done to laugh, except in the nursery, and I was continually being scolded for being in a hurry, running and upsetting food, instead of acting with dignity and decorum. One day, proud to be allowed to join the adults in the dining room, with the Old Masters on the walls, the Brussels carpet beneath my feet and grown up lunch on the table, I was reduced to tears by my mother's saying casually to the governess,

'After all, eight is very young and babyish.'

Even when I was seventeen, she suddenly pinched my arm at dinner in London because of something I said that had annoyed her.

'I was only trying to make conversation,' I protested.

'You do not make conversation with your mother!' she replied.

Yet all the staff loved Mama and she was very fond of them. When Mrs Jenks came up to my mother in bed or at her desk, Mama called her, 'my little Annie.' None of the servants left voluntarily and though my mother never told Mr Copper how much she valued him, he must have been aware of it. It would never have occurred to him to seek another position.

Mama was respected by all the estate workers and villagers. However austere she might be, everyone looked forward to her annual appearance at the winter concert, with songs and tableaux, in the Roger Gillingham Charity School in the village. She always looked her staff straight in the eye and they knew where they stood with her.

Though Mama had no husband or lover, she had many friends who, once gained, were hers for life. A stockbroker, John Dudley Ryder, gave her comfort and moral support in her pregnancy. When my father, being embarrassed by her enormous size, would not accompany her to the theatre, Ryder willingly acted as her escort.

Daphne and I gleefully watched our mother's visitors vying for her attention. Their visits also meant that we could use the marble stairs when we accompanied a guest up to his or her room – a rare event. She would never allow us to have any of our own friends to stay, however, so that I was greatly embarrassed on a visit to Derby for balls and the races, to hear

my hostess boasting that she would soon be staying at
Kingston Lacy with Viola. The next best thing was to enjoy
the company of our mother's friends, who were all
exceptional people.

Whole troops of actors and actresses would be invited to
Kingston Lacy when they were performing at Bournemouth.
Ellen Terry was sixty-five when I met her, but still lovely to
look upon, with great dignity, a kindly smile and dim, blue
eyes. She walked into the Saloon to see the pictures, lifting
her head and gazing all round, speaking with an actress's
very clear diction. I pestered her for her autograph, which she
wrote for me, in her big, shaky handwriting, adding,
'Farewell. God knows if we shall meet again.'

We never did.

Diplomats were frequent guests at Kingston Lacy. We were
warned not to go too near the Portuguese Ambassador to the
Court of Brussels in case we tripped and fell against him.
He had two cork legs, a wig, artificial teeth and only
half a left hand which he kept in his pocket. Ugly though he
was, he had great charm. He lost his bachelor state inadvertently, when a lady with whom he had been involved in a
serious road accident misconstrued his expressions of solici-
tude and thought he was proposing to her.

Count Wolf Metternich, the German Ambassador, was
keen on protocol and quite remote from us children. I can
remember only that when we were motoring with him in
an open car, his hat blew off. When the chauffeur went to
pick it up and handed it back, his excellency refused to put
it back on his head, throwing it disdainfully away.

Mother carefully instructed us in how to behave when
guests were present, so that we gradually lost our shyness.

'Now when someone comes into the room for the first
time, get up! Don't sit there. Get up and shake hands, smile

and look them in the eyes when you speak to them. Don't look away.'

Ralph remained impervious to her training, always staying silent even when his own friends were present. Only occasionally would something amuse him into embarrassingly loud utterance.

'Here comes Queen Victoria!' he suddenly announced when our mother's best friend, Marie Belloc Lowndes, the novelist, arrived swathed in black and wearing a bonnet with a black ostrich plume.

I was placed next to guests at lunch in order to practise my conversational arts and was delighted when, occasionally, I scored a success. When Frank Dicksee, President of the Royal Academy, tall and slender, with a grey beard like a Van Dyke portrait, asked if my mother remembered seeing his picture in any academy show, seeing my mother nonplussed, I stepped gallantly into the breach, piping up:

'Yes, yes, I saw it! It was a lovely picture of a little girl in the middle of a garden of lilies.' I was right, for the picture had been painted at the request of two friends of his when their fourteen-year-old daughter had died. Mr Dicksee was very gratified that I remembered it. Usually, however, Mama would say lightly,

'Don't take any notice of Cissie. She doesn't know what she is talking about.'

Sadly, I was slow to learn when to keep judiciously quiet. One day we went to lunch with our father's cousin, Sir John Bankes, who lived to be ninety-one and was first a High Court Judge, then a Lord of Appeal. Listening to a boring conversation between him and my mother, I suddenly heard Ralph's name mentioned, he being then at Eton.

'Is the boy good at football?' – a judicial, Sherlock Holmesian question, though I did not realise it.

'Oh, yes!' said my mother.

'Oh, no!' said I. 'He hates it. He told me!' ignoring warning signs sent to me by Daphne.

'Indeed!' remarked cousin John significantly, deducing that Ralph was assuredly shaping up to be a homosexual. This was quite untrue, although Ralph never did like football, and though, when still a ward in Chancery, with cousin John as guardian, he shielded another boy in a school scandal.

One advantage of Mama's frequently having artists to stay was that one often had one's portrait painted. Mary Gow, with iron-grey hair scraped back in a bun and *pince nez*, whose water colours were much prized by Americans, later painted me from memory, as I had been as a very young girl with my hair down.

'I remember you very well. Your eyes were so blue, dear,' she said, lovingly, though, in fact, they were green or hazel.

Taking a proprietory interest in the career of one shy, childlike artist, R. J. Eves, I determined to find famous men for him to paint. One day, donning my leather helmet, I rode off behind Ralph on his motor bike to call on Thomas Hardy at Max Gate and invite him and his wife to tea. The bait of Kingston Lacy proved irresistible and Hardy, though having then the reputaton of being antisocial, accepted my invitation with alacrity.

My plan was successful. Eves and Hardy liked one another straight away and became firm friends. A portrait which results from their friendship hangs in the National Portrait Gallery. Hardy was charming company, and obligingly let Daphne take a photograph of him on the lawn. Wanting to impress him, I told him I was reading *Jude the Obscure*.

'That is far too depressing for you at your age,' he said, with kindly interest.

Though no father was present to help us when visitors came, we nearly always had our father's white-moustached uncle, great uncle Albert, Squire of Wolfeton near Dorchester, who was easy-going, cheerful and totally undemanding.

Throughout our adolescence, Mama was most conscientious about giving us a wide education. She took a suite of rooms for long periods at the Hotel Wagram in Paris, engaging a French governess and French teachers for us, allowing us to shop at a famous hat shop and to experience having Parisian dresses specially made. At the hotel, she taught us to maintain a courteous and dignified relationship with the other guests. Only once did she lose her own dignity. Finding an army of ants moving through her lingerie in search of a half-eaten box of caramels which I had left in her bedroom, she hurled an exclusive Bond Street corset through the hotel window, no doubt to be salvaged next morning by the deserving poor.

Unfortunately, by the time we were seventeen, Mama had tired of us. She stopped meeting us regularly for lunch at Stewart's in Bond Street on Saturdays to give the servants a rest, and taking us once a week to Selfridges for a one and sixpence manicure. Walking in London with Daphne and me made her feel, she said unkindly, like 'un âne à deux paniers'!

Gone were the days when we leant up against her stiff, crackling taffeta blouse as she put her arm tenderly round us. She did not even wish to see us, but would lunch alone at one o'clock in the dining room, on a tray brought in by the butler. Daphne and I would have our meal later, at half past one, after she had left the room.

The deep-rooted cause of Mama's irritation was, of course, that we remained unmarried. She was unashamedly acquisitive and expected the same of us.

'Tell him it's your birthday today,' she said more than once, when we lunched with Lockett Agnew, head of the firm in Bond Street, knowing that he would buy me a gift. Yet titles mattered even more than riches. She refused to let us be bridesmaids for Violette Selfridge, even though the presents would have been magnificent. Our husbands would have to be both rich and well-connected to please her.

We therefore always felt slightly constrained at the balls she gave for us. My unease in a ball room had begun at a very early age in London when Mrs Wordsworth, queen of dance teachers, portly and pompous in black bombazine, with a black jet necklace and black sequins bobbing up and down on her mighty bosom, had fixed me with her one good and one glass eye and commanded, 'Darling child, come and dance with me.' Mama's presence and fearsome expectations at our own balls were no less daunting. She would invite only beautiful girls and eligible men – young guardsmen who had survived the Great War. Men brought by mothers and daughters would be scrutinised severely.

Once my mother put out her beringed hand (she had a set of emeralds, ring, bracelets and necklace which she wore at balls) and stopped me and my unlucky partner as we danced past her, I in layer upon of layer of pink silk with a bunch of rosebuds at the waist.

'Goodbye!' she said.

'But I'm not going,' replied my partner.

'Oh, yes, you are!' said Mama, and off he went. The mother of the girl who had brought him telephoned in a rage, but next day the papers had photographs of him involved in a swindle.

Years after my expulsion from Brook Street and Kingston Lacy, by accident, I encountered my mother in a London book shop. I stood in front of her, waiting for her to speak.

'Who are you?' she asked.

'I'm your daughter, Cis,' I said.

'Well, don't forget me quite,' she replied, and swept out of the shop. Without a kiss or a handshake, we went our separate ways.

Postscript

The end of our childhood coincided with the end of the First World War. We had been only slightly involved in the 'war effort', helping at charity bazaars in London and at a canteen for Australian servicemen. We had also each adopted a lonely soldier to whom to write and send parcels of food and chocolate. Otherwise the war had made little difference to our lives. *Thé dansants* continued to be held. Our deprivations were of an extremely trivial order — attending a garden party at Buckingham Palace instead of being formally presented to the King, and making do with lemonade and walnuts at a ball instead of grander fare. Yet we still had regularly sent up to London by Boast the keeper, teal, wild duck, rabbits and an occasional hare.

We knew how privileged we were to be safe in England. One of Daphne's close friends, smiling, fair-haired Noel Durrent, had been killed in the trenches. Of all the young gardeners and menservants from Kingston Lacy who had joined the Dorset Yeomanry and seen service in the Dardanelles, few returned. At Kingston Lacy, action was constantly expected but never materialised.

''Em 'ave been 'ere tonight, Ed,' said old Hart, poking his head round the mushroom house to speak to the head gardener's boy one morning in 1914. The noises and flares he had witnessed had, however, been caused not by Zeppelins but only by a large fire in the offices.

Gradually, life returned to normal. After our London *début*, Daphne and I plunged into the hospitable world of country house parties where, without the protection of Mama, we had to learn to converse sensibly with people of all ages, famous or not. It was a great embarrassment to us that we could not return this hospitality. Sadly and unfairly, only Ralph was allowed to invite guests to stay at Kingston Lacy.

Daphne and I increased in confidence and our ties with Kingston Lacy and with each other began gradually to slacken. We visited Ralph at Oxford for 'Commem' balls, punting with him and our Dorset neighbour, Jack (later Sir John) Hanham on the river next morning, but we remembered Jack as he had been as a child, climbing the trees and running about the park in an impractical green velvet suit with a lace collar. Boys with whom we had grown up, we decided, were just not exciting!

My father had left me £1,000 a year, reduced, by inattention, to £700. Gathering round me more and more interesting friends of whom my mother could never approve, I began to taste the delicious fruits of independence. It was time for me to go my own way and to leave Brook Street and Kingston Lacy, where I was a constant source of irritation. My mother made that perfectly clear!

For a few exotic years I sampled student life in post-war Paris, skied, bob-sleighed and skated at St. Moritz and joined Daphne, briefly, in Florence, where, missing my company, she had gone to learn singing. I sampled the delights of Venice – its dignified antiquity as well as its outrageous modern gaiety and extravagance. My base was however always London where first I had my own service flat in Old Burlington Street, filled with the fragrance of hyacinths in winter and lilies in summer, so that one of my innumerable men friends once almost fainted. I next acquired a flat in Grosvenor St whose two-hundred-year-old floor groaned under the dance I immediately gave for fifty people.

The gloss of girlhood – so brief, so glamorous – turned, inevitably, after those few, heady years, to the matronly measure of marriage. My engagement to a doctor from Australia set the seal upon my mother's disapproval and rejection of me. She did not attend my wedding.

My husband's first concern was to pay my debts, for my inherited extravagant tastes had been left uncurbed by the over-chivalrous Bank. Bills from Covent Garden and accounts for dresses and hats continued to pour in before I learned that money has to be increased before it can be spent. I simply forgot several valuable furs stored in Gorringes in Buckingham Palace Road, which were sold after the statutory seven years.

My mother never received my husband or asked to see my two daughters, Lalage and Fay. As well as the wrought iron gates of Kingston Lacy, the elegant front door of 61, Brook Street, which became her permanent home when she handed over her Dorset responsibilities to Ralph and his wife, remained closed to me and mine for ever.

'I suppose you know Mummy died,' wrote Daphne in 1953, thirteen days after the funeral. Our mother had died in London on November the 29th.

Ralph evidently saw no reason to disagree with Mama's decision to banish me from the family home, for I never heard from him again after he had given me away at my wedding. My letters to him remained unanswered. He proved a popular and considerate Squire, who valued his tenants and never raised their rents, making careful provision for them in his will and ensuring, by his legacy of Kingston Lacy to the National Trust, that it would be carefully looked after.

I heard from time to time from Daphne, though I did not know until some years after her death from a heart attack that she had driven an ambulance during World War Two. She lived for the latter part of her life in a cottage in the grounds of the Manor House at Studland, after the house itself had become a hotel. When she died, Ralph ordered that none of her things should be touched. All must remain exactly as she had left them.

It is, however, to my mother that my thoughts return as I stand again in front of the stately mansion which was my home so many years ago. Her last recorded words on a visit to Kingston Lacy during World War Two were addressed to the rueful head gardener. A red brick American hospital squatted in the carefully tended Park; his tenderly nurtured flower garden had been turned over to vegetables for the War Effort; his fine collection of orchids ousted by cucumbers.

Still stately in her black dress and carrying her black parasol, Mama strode down the Lady's Walk and entered the garden. Ralph was then master of Kingston Lacy, having after passing with distinction his examinations at Eton, Oxford and in Law School, settled down contentedly to a quiet country life with his wife and two children. Nevertheless, my mother took it for granted, just as she used to do, that Mr Dukes would magically appear from his six acres the instant she called, 'Dukes! Dukes!'

'Where have you been? You aren't about!' she said, as she always had done, when the head gardener, busy with some plants, straightened himself, brushed off the dust and came to stand before her, giving her a less than cheerful greeting.

'Never mind, Dukes! Keep your pecker up!' she exhorted

him, 'We shall win!'

Even in old age, and at the height of the war, Mama remained as proudly indomitable as ever.